William Steuart Trench and his management of the Digby estate, King's County, 1857–71

Maynooth Studies in Local History

SERIES EDITOR Raymond Gillespie

This year, Maynooth Studies in Local History publishes its 100th study. Over the twenty years of the series these short books have ranged widely, both chronologically and geographically, over the local experience in the Irish past. They have demonstrated the vitality of the study of local history in Ireland and have shown the range of possibilities open to anyone interested in studying local history. From medieval Dalkey to Granard in the 1950s, past volumes in this series have dissected the local experience in the complex and contested social worlds of which it is part. Perhaps inevitably, many have concentrated on well-established paths of enquiry with works on the Famine of the 1840s and the late 19th-century land war, while others reveal the riches that await gathering from the medieval and early modern worlds. The sister series, Maynooth Research Guides in Local History, has also facilitated access to these worlds by providing reliable and user-friendly resources that help those unfamiliar with the raw evidence to deal with the sometimes difficult sources that survive from the more remote past. Studies of local worlds over such long periods are vital for the future since they not only stretch the historical imagination but provide a longer perspective on the evolution of local societies in Ireland and help us to understand more fully the complex evolution of the Irish experience. The existence of a large body of published studies, which are not a simple chronicling of events relating to an area within administrative or geographically determined boundaries, opens the possibility of comparative study to allow us to see better why particular regions had their own personality in the past. Such an exercise is clearly one of the most exciting challenges for the future.

Like previous volumes in the series, the six short books published as part of this centenary offering are reconstructions of the socially diverse worlds of the poor as well as the rich, women as well as men, and reconstruct the way in which those who inhabited those worlds lived their daily lives, often little affected by the large themes that dominate the writing of national history. In addressing these issues, studies such as those presented in these short books, are at the forefront of Irish historical research and represent some of the most innovative and exciting work being undertaken in Irish history today. They also provide models that others can follow up and adapt in their own studies of the Irish past. In such ways will we understand better the regional diversity of Ireland and the social and cultural basis for that diversity. These books convey the vibrancy and excitement of the world of Irish local history today.

Maynooth Studies in Local History: Number 101

William Steuart Trench and his management of the Digby estate, King's County, 1857–71

Mary Delaney

FOUR COURTS PRESS

Set in 10pt on 12pt Bembo by
Carrigboy Typesetting Services for
FOUR COURTS PRESS LTD
7 Malpas Street, Dublin 8, Ireland
www.fourcourtspress.ie
and in North America for
FOUR COURTS PRESS
c/o ISBS, 920 N.E. 58th Avenue, Suite 300, Portland, OR 97213.

ISBN 978-1-84682-353-4

Printed in England by
Antony Rowe Ltd, Chippenham, Wilts.

Contents

Acknowledgments

I wish to acknowledge with gratitude some of the many people who encouraged and assisted me to complete this work. I am indebted to Lord Edward Digby of Minterne, Dorset, England, who welcomed me into his home and gave me access to the family's collection of private papers on Geashill which has greatly enriched this work. I wish to express my sincere thanks to Dr Terence Dooley, my MA supervisor, for his encouragement, support and helpful suggestions, and to Professor Raymond Gillespie and Mr Rob Goodbody of the Department of Modern History, NUI Maynooth. I would like to thank my good friend, Martina Behan, for all her advice and assistance throughout my research and for her help in proof reading my manuscript. John Kearney, Michael Byrne and the staff of the Offaly Historical and Archaeological Society in Tullamore helped with my many queries. The support and friendship of my fellow students in the MA class at NUIM was greatly appreciated. Finally, I would like to dedicate this work to my aunt, the late Alice Smyth, who was Postmistress in Geashill for many years, for her inspiration in kindling my interest in the Digby estate and who sadly passed away during the completion of this work.

Introduction

The period in Ireland between the Famine and the Land War has been described as a 'golden age of capitalism'.[1] For many the mid-Victorian period was one of great economic expansion and prosperity. This is reflected in the works of Comerford, Cullen, Donnelly, Dooley and Vaughan[2]. The 1851 Census revealed that the majority of Irish people still lived in the countryside. In fact, 83 per cent of Irish dwellers were rural and were dependent on the land. In the 19th century, Irish land was owned by landlords who played a pivotal role in shaping the rural fabric of the country and landlord–tenant relationships came to dominate the mid-Victorian period. Some landowners had small estates between 2,000 and 5,000 acres while others like the duke of Leinster owned 73,000 acres and the marquis of Downshire had an estate of 115,000 acres.[3] Regardless of estate size landlords exercised enormous social, political and economic power in their respective localities.[4] The physical presence of their 'big' houses surrounded by splendid demesnes, which dominated the Irish rural landscape, was symbolic of this power.

By 1851, many tenant holdings on these estates were still small, often less than 15 acres. By 1861, however, 40 per cent of the country was held in farms of 100 acres and over.[5] The second half of the 19th century thus witnessed a rapid change in both the physical condition of the landscape and the composition of the rural population. On many estates land quality and living conditions improved for the rural dweller. But such improvements came at a cost to the lower end of society, especially the landless labourers, whose numbers declined by almost a third between 1851 and 1901. This reduction can be attributed to the policy of consolidation and improvement carried out by many Irish landlords. By 1851 there were around 10,000 landlords in Ireland. Over 75 per cent of them were either resident on their estate or resided elsewhere in the country,[6] the remaining 25 per cent were absentee, who appointed agents to manage their Irish estates. The agent was more than just a collector of rent; he was also expected to fulfil duties such as the providing of relief and employment as well as having responsibility for both the physical and management maintenance of the estate. However, as the 19th century progressed many were professional land agents, who took on additional duties of magistrate, architect and engineer. History casts a dark shadow on many of them and while the landlords were sometimes remembered as decent men, the agents were loathed by many. In fact in one folktale on the Lansdowne estate, they were described as 'devils one and all'.[7]

This work sets out to examine the agency of William Steuart Trench on the Digby estate in Geashill in King's County from 1857 to 1871. Trench came from a new school of agents and had previously worked on estates in counties Monaghan and Kerry, where he is remembered by contemporary writers and in local folklore as a tyrant. During his agency in Kenmare one observer described him as 'a haughty tyrant, blustering and crimpling all the joys and comforts, social and economic'.[8] The physical legacy of Trench's time in Geashill appears to be a positive one. Under his agency the estate was transformed from bleakness and poverty to one with good productive land, where many tenants enjoyed an improved living standard and where improvements in housing and land quality gained national and indeed international recognition. However, like elsewhere in Ireland, not all tenants on the Digby estate shared in this golden age of prosperity.

Gerard Lyne's work has documented Trench's agency on the Lansdowne estate in Co. Kerry[9] and his time on both the Shirley and Bath estates in Co. Monaghan is discussed in works by Patrick Duffy.[10] However, little detailed work has been published on Trench's agency at Geashill. The Digby private papers are the main primary source used in this research. They are in a private collection in Dorset, England, and include letters, newspaper articles, photographs and a water-colour sketch album of cottages on the estate where improvements took place.[11] The most relevant of all the material are the annual reports sent from William Trench to Lord Digby.[12] These reports are invaluable as they allow the reader to create a vivid picture of life on the Geashill estate. One can therefore evaluate Trench's style of management and the transformations experienced by the people of the locality on an annual basis. So what then were the 'true' realities on Lord Digby's estate from 1857 to 1871? Contemporary primary sources such as Godkin's *Land War in Ireland* as well as Trench's own work, *Realities of Irish life*, are greatly bolstered by the private collection of previously unpublished material in an attempt to answer this question. The first chapter will examine the appointment of William Steuart Trench and his son Thomas Weldon Trench as agents and will provide a clear description of the Digby estate in 1857. The second chapter will evaluate the role of W.S. Trench as he dealt with the problems of lease-breaking, subdivision of land, tenants in arrears and the threat of Ribbonism. Improvements carried out on the estate, especially those in land drainage and cottage design will be examined in the third chapter. The final chapter will assess the impact such improvements had on the local community. It will examine Thomas Weldon Trench's treatment of a 79-year-old beggar named Alice Dillon. In the conclusion it is hoped to ascertain what the 'actual realities' were on the estate at Geashill and assess the validity of Trench's impression, that 'Lord Digby and those who worked under him can look back with pleasure at having achieved a moral victory over what at one time appeared as dangerous and uncompromising a subject as any Irish landlord or land agent could possibly undertake to manage'.[13]

1. The Digbys and the appointment of William Steuart Trench

William Steuart Trench, the youngest of 15 children, was born in 1808 near Ballybrittas in the Queen's County.[1] He was christened Richard. His older brother William died in infancy in 1803 and anxious to maintain William as a family name, Richard became known as William Steuart. His father, Thomas, was the Church of Ireland dean of Kildare and his mother was the daughter of Walter Weldon of Rahinderry, Queen's County, who was a member of parliament. He was educated at the Royal School in Armagh and Trinity College, Dublin. In 1832 he married Elizabeth Sealy Townsend, whose father was the Master of Chancery in Ireland at the time.[2] They had one daughter Anna Maria, born in 1836, and two sons, Thomas Weldon born in 1833 and John Townsend born in 1834. Trench for most of his adult life was employed as a professional land agent, a position for which he considered himself well qualified. He claimed in his *Realities of Irish life* 'to have lost no opportunity of acquiring information which might qualify me to become a land agent as being the most suitable in its higher branches to my capacity'.[3] The traditional duties of a land agent involved the collecting of rents, the letting of land and quite often the evicting of tenants. However, both Trench and his two sons came to represent a new type of agent, one who was far more versatile and multi-functional, taking on the roles of magistrate, architect and accountant, among others. Such duties were even more significant when the landlord did not live on his estate. Land agents were recruited not only from the ranks of the legal profession but also from the landed gentry and many agents purchased or inherited landed property themselves.[4] William Trench owned some property in Cardtown in the Slieve Bloom Mountains in Queen's County, which he acquired in 1843. He was involved in carrying out land reclamation and began extensive potato cultivation on his property which proved very profitable. However, the blight of the 1840s lost him his fortune and it is thought that this shaped his attitude to Irish rural poverty and perhaps instilled in him bitterness towards the poorer classes.[5] An Oxford professor visited Trench's home in Cardtown, near Mountrath on 26 September, 1852 and observed that the fields on his estate were large and well drained. He saw no cabins and met scarcely a single person and commented that 'there seems to be neither poverty nor overpopulation'. Trench explained to him how he had reclaimed over 600 acres of land at a cost of £14 per acre but in the aftermath of the famine such improvements came to a halt.[6]

Many of Trench's relatives were also employed as agents throughout the country: his cousin, Benjamin Bloomfield Trench worked as agent to Charles Verner (1854) and was also agent on the Bath estate 1868–75.[7] George Trench was employed on the Talbot-Crosbie estate in Co. Kerry while his cousin, William Trench, acted as agent on the Heywood estate in Queen's County. Other members of the Trench family held important positions in the church, for example Richard Chenevix Trench, who was archbishop of Dublin from 1864 to 1884.[8] Prior to his appointment as agent for Lord Digby, William Steuart Trench had been employed in Co. Monaghan, on both the Bath and Shirley estates. He also acted as agent on the extensive estates of the marquess of Lansdowne in Co. Kerry. On both estates in Monaghan he was noted for the implementation of assisted emigration schemes or what he referred to as 'voluntary' emigration. For example Patrick Duffy has noted in his work on assisted emigration from the Shirley estate, that by 1851 the flow of assisted emigrants was reduced to a trickle, however, that year marked the beginning of a significant outflow of assisted emigrants from the neighbouring Bath state, under the agency of William Steuart Trench.[9] Similar schemes were carried out while Trench worked in Kenmare, Co. Kerry, where he helped to ship over 4,000 destitute people to the United States and Canada. Trench looked upon such schemes as a cheap and efficient way to improve the estate. It seemed that on the Shirley estate the idea behind Trench's policies was that impoverished tenants on tiny holdings, who were in rent arrears with little possibility of paying any rent, should be encouraged to give up their farms and be given their passage to emigrate. This would reduce future changes in rates, consolidate holdings, and improve the life of the people themselves.[10]

If the latter is true, then the memory of Trench should be a positive one. However, the works of poets such as Patrick Kavanagh paint a dark picture of Trench. For example, he tells how when Trench died, the rats devoured his corpse before it could be buried. He also refers to Trench and his son in one of his poems as 'those haters of the Celtic race'.[11] Hostilities towards Trench also existed in the folk tales of Kenmare, where in 1858 a local man described Trench as 'one of the meanest and most contemptible petty tyrants that ever held authority over poor mortals'. Gerard Lyne in his work on the Lansdowne estate records how Charles Russell, lord chief justice of England, visiting Kenmare in 1880, reflected on local attitudes to the memory of late W.S. Trench: 'No kindly recollection of the late Mr Trench seems to survive and no kindly feeling towards his son, the present agent seems to exist'.[12] The Trenches are remembered in much the same way by the people of Geashill. A local man, Thomas Davis, remembers a rhyme told by his grandmother.

> There's grace on the pulpit
> There's wit on the bench
> But there's nothing but dirt,
> Can be found on a Trench.[13]

From such stories it is fair to say that the Trenches exercised significant control over the lives of their tenants, not only economically but also socially. It is claimed that in both Monaghan and Kerry no tenant could marry without the consent of Trench. This is reflected in a ballad from the Shirley Estate:

> Oh Girls of Farney it is true,
> That each true hearted wench
> Before she weds, must get consent
> From Pious Father Trench.[14]

Early marriages led to more children and subsequently worsened the problem of sub-division. If the marriage rule was breached, the tenant was usually evicted as a punishment. A common trait displayed by the Trenches in their management tactics was their use of a wide network of spies, or what Patrick Duffy refers to as a system of 'local espionage, called keepers'.[15] Local people were engaged to spy on their neighbouring tenants. This system, while effective from Trench's point of view, divided the local community. Folklore may not be kind to Trench but a more positive aspect of his agency is reflected in the improvements carried out on the estates he managed. He transformed the town of Kenmare by improving the dwelling houses of the tenantry, raising the standard of farming, improving local services and developing local industries and fishing. He had similar plans for the Shirley estate but he was not allowed to pursue those, leading him to resign his agency. It may well have been Trench's previous experience at reclamation and land improvement that convinced the then Lord Digby to engage his services at Geashill. Edward St Vincent Digby was the grandson of Thomas Coke of Norfolk, who was noted for his contribution to the agricultural revolution in Britain in the 18th century. Like his grandfather, he was interested in renovating the appearance and improving the quality of the lands at Geashill. When William Steuart Trench was appointed to manage the estate he installed his eldest son, Thomas Weldon Trench, as co-agent, establishing his residence at Geashill Manor, where successive agents had lived, including Richard Digby, John Digby and David Thompson.[16]

William Trench was appointed agent to the Digby estate in 1857. King's County in the middle of 19th century consisted of twelve baronies.[17] Like elsewhere in Ireland, landownership patterns in King's County indicate a great diversity in both acreage and valuation. The Digby estate, however, was the largest in the county and consisted of 31,000 acres. It comprised the entire barony of Geashill and part of the former monastic lands of Killeigh. The estate lay to the west and south of the barony of Philipstown and to the east of the baronies of Ballycowen and Ballyboy, while to the south, it shared a boundary with Queen's County. Geashill comprised 6 per cent of the total land area of King's County and was located approximately 51 miles from Dublin, on the

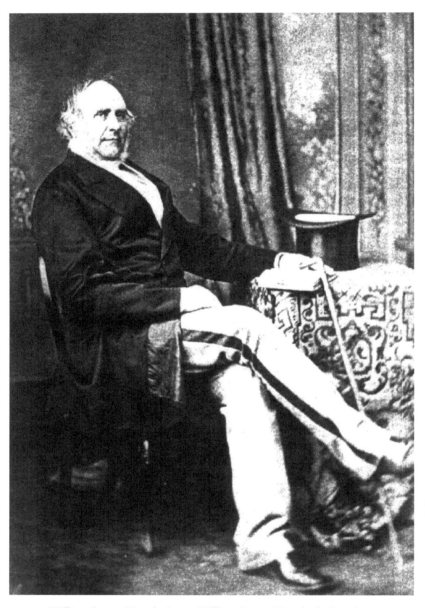

1 William Steuart Trench. *Source:* William Steuart Trench, the Lansdowne estate in Co. Kerry

road from Portarlington to Tullamore.[18] It formed part of the Gaelic Ui Failghe territory and was controlled by the O'Connors until the 17th century. Topographically, it was drained by both the Tullamore and Clodiagh Rivers, the relief of the land varying from 61 metres in the north to over 122 metres in the south; some of which consisted of bogland and fluvio-glacial deposits of eskers. In fact, Trench described 5,000 acres as 'deep red bog'.[19] The remainder consisted of profitable land comprising arable, pasture and wood.

The Digby family resided in Sherbourne and Minterne in Dorset, England. They derived their title to the estate from Lettice Fitzgerald, the daughter of Gerard, Lord Offaly, who was the eldest son of the 11th earl of Kildare. Her mother, Lady Catherine Knollys was a cousin of Queen Elizabeth I.[20] When her grandfather died, being female she could not inherit the earldom but she was made a peeress in her own right and was given the title of Lady Offaly. Lettice married Sir Robert Digby of Coleshill in Warwickshire in 1598. Sir Robert had been knighted in 1596 by the earl of Essex in Dublin. He was returned to parliament as member for Athy in 1613. Until his death in 1618 the couple resided at Geashill Castle and she laid claim to the lands in the barony of Geashill. However, dispute arose and dragged on for so long that James I decided to adjudicate in person. In order to settle the difference he created her baroness of Offaly in 1619[21] and her heirs were granted the manor of Geashill and the former monastic lands of Killeigh. During the rising of the 1640s there were many attempts by local families such as the O'Dempseys and the O'Connors to besiege her castle. During one such attempt, one of her sons fell into the hands of the enemy and was brought under the castle walls in chains, threatening that unless she surrendered at once, they would strike his head off before her eyes. However, it seems that Lettice was a very spirited lady and was not dismayed by such threats, replying that she had a Roman Catholic clergyman behind the walls of her castle and that his life would be immediately forfeited if they dared to touch a hair on her son's head.[22] The enemies withdrew at once. After further attempts to besiege her home at Geashill, Lady Digby returned to Coleshire, where she resided until her death in 1658[23] and her epitaph written by herself reads,

> Lettice lived eighteen years a virgin pure
> Twenty years wedded happy and secure
> Then death deprived her of her dearest friend
> Whose constant widow she lived to her end.[64]

Following her death, her eldest son, Robert Digby inherited the lands at Geashill. The estate continued in the hands of the Digbys for the next two centuries. On 12 May 1856, Edward, 8th Baron and 2nd Earl Digby, died. It seems he was a very *laissez faire* landlord, residing in his splendid residence at Sherbourne, and 'having full command of all that wealth could give'.[25] He rarely visited Geashill and granted tenants very long leases. However, because these grants extended beyond his own life-time, he was deemed to have exceeded his legal powers. This would prove to be a problem for his successor and in particular for William Trench who was given the task of sorting out the estate. Edward Digby died unmarried and so his titles died with him.[26] His estate at Geashill passed to his cousin Edward St Vincent, the 9th Baron Digby. The new owner felt that his late ancestor had 'no right, moral or legal, to lease away his Irish lands for two thirds of their real value'.[27] The new landlord was therefore determined to break the leases which his predecessor had granted. This was to create much anxiety and upheaval at Geashill, where the tenants were faced with loss of holding, which they previously considered secure. Acting upon his legal rights, the 9th Lord Digby embarked upon breaking these leases, leading the tenants to look to executors for redress and compensation. It was in the midst of this dispute that William Trench's services were engaged.

The Trenches were granted full powers to act on behalf of Baron Digby, as is evident from the deed of contract drawn up between the Right Hon. Edward St Vincent Digby and William Stewart Trench and Thomas Weldon Trench in September 1857: 'I hereby make constitute and appoint William Stewart Trench and Thomas Weldon Trench to be my true and lawful attorneys and attorney for me and in my name'.[28] One must examine the challenges faced by the new agents at Geashill and the policies they subsequently enacted. Did their agency reflect their previous management techniques executed in Co. Monaghan and on the Lansdowne estate in Co. Kerry?

Trench took up his appointment at Geashill on 1 June 1857. Accompanied by his son, he spent the first few weeks assessing the situation. Their impression of the lands at Geashill was not a positive one and reflects earlier descriptions by Coote and Lewis. The village was described by Charles Coote in 1801 as 'an inconsiderable village, mostly composed of thatched cabins'. It was also noted for having 'the best pig fair in the province if not in the kingdom'.[29] The village had a distinctive triangular shape as can be seen from Larkin's collection of maps for King's County.[30] In 1837, Samuel Lewis gave a similar description of the village adding that it had a constabulary police station, a dispensary and a patent for a market.[31]

In the 1857 report sent to Lord Digby, Trench describes the estate as 'one of the most wretched and discouraging in Ireland'.[32] He records that there were 889 tenants on the estate, 1,163 houses and that the estate had a population of 6,192. Annual rent amounted to £15,000, but the amount of arrears was £40,948.[33] In the same report, Trench gave a clear description of the condition of the estate, including a breakdown of the quality of the land. He described it as being a broad plain with upland, and extensive valleys of flat moors of deep red bog. It had a general elevation of 250 to 350 feet above

2 Sketch illustrating the attitude of the tenants on the Digby estate, 1857.
Source: 1857 Annual Report from Trench to Lord Digby

sea level. He commented that 'very few spots indeed were suitable for finishing either a bullock or a heifer'.[34] He saw potential in the moorlands by the Tullamore River: 'If these were cultivated and manured they could produce large yields of crops and hay'.[35] However, substantial portions of the land comprised cutaway bog which was extremely wet. He also noted the considerable forests and blackthorn hedges, which added to the warmth of the landscape. He recommended that the wet moors be drained and pointed out to Lord Digby that this would be a good investment for the future. Trench displayed great foresight in his proposals for land reclamation as many of his ideas are features of modern-day farming in the locality. He suggested that a sum of £500–£1,000 be set aside for it annually and that a proper engineer, such as the local man Henry Millie, be employed to oversee the work.[36] The value of livestock on the estate (valued in 1866) was £52,295, while the value of crops was £54,479. He suggested to Lord Digby that there was a need to consolidate the farms on the estate: 'by removing the worst characters or weeding them out and to add their land to the farms of the most improving tenants' as he had done on the Bath and Lansdowne estates.[37] His plans lead one to question: what became of these 'worst characters'?

He also included his observations on the general condition of the dwelling houses of the ordinary tenants, as well as the attitude of the people on the estate: 'buildings presented the worst appearance of all; many of them were modern ruins'.[38] He went on to say 'Fifty to one hundred years previous to that there seemed to have been unsuccessful attempts at improving them but since then everything has slept. An ancient ruin all men of taste admires, but a modern ruin is a painful spectacle'.[39] He described the attitudes of the tenants as conservative and indifferent, saying that the only wish of the district was to 'let us alone',[40] as illustrated in a sketch sent from Trench to Lord Digby (figure 2). He made reference to the road network of the area and concluded that it was in a very poor state. Many old roads were badly mended, with deep dykes filled with water running alongside them. It seemed that little attempt had been made to update the roads in the area since Skinner and Taylor had surveyed them in 1777.[41] There was no direct road from Geashill to Tullamore in 1777, and apparently this was the case until the 1850s. Trench acknowledged that some new roads were under construction, but pointed out that many of these were of no value.[42] The exception to this was a road under construction that crossed the Tullamore River and linked Tullamore to Geashill, connecting with the Ballinagar road. He described this as 'a road of value'.[43] This was probably due to Tullamore being the main trading town in the area, as well as housing the county gaol and court house and being a major transport route on the Grand Canal. He saw roads as vital to any future improvements to the area and recommended that they should be kept in good repair. However, he concluded that they should be funded by the rate payers. Trench and his son, Thomas Townsend, understood the importance of education while working in Kenmare and may have promoted it there. However, how much of this was due to the Trenches was debatable as the 3rd marquess of Lansdowne was noted for his interest in national education.[44]

When examining educational facilities in Geashill, Trench reported that there were nine schools in total on the estate in 1857, six of which were national schools, the remaining three were under the Church Education Society.[45] In 1831 the British government began to fund primary schools, which were called national schools. It was hoped that children from all religious denominations would attend. Unhappy with the national school system, the established church set up the Church Education Society in 1839 as an alternative to national schools. Trench reported that regrettably, most of the national schools in the barony had fallen under the control of the Roman Catholics. There was no national school in Geashill village except a Church Education school, where the people had no confidence in the headmaster. The majority of children attended school in a miserable mud cabin, located outside the village. Trench recommended to Lord Digby that there was a need to build a new national school in the village of Geashill. If Lord Digby provided a free site, the commissioners of education would provide a half to two-thirds of the cost. This would greatly benefit the barony.[46] If Trench and his son were to carry out improvements with any success, then the first step was to build offices and houses on good size farms. He recommended that Lord Digby should not

3 Sketch of Geashill National School in 1857.
Source: 1857 Annual Report to Lord Digby

increase the rents on these premises as this could cause resentment, but suggested that others in the community would see the benefit and want to follow suit.[47]

While W.S. Trench's observations and recommendations for the Digby estate laid out the problems of improving the physical landscape, a far more challenging task faced him; that of managing the tenantry at Geashill. His first task here was to request Mr Thompson, the former agent to provide a statement of arrears due by each tenant to the late earl up to the end of March 1856, together with details of how much had been paid to the office since then. The sum of the total arrears due to that date was £40,948 17s. Of that, £7,074 10s. 1d. had been paid, £162 8s. 3d. was abandoned, leaving a deficit of £33,711 19s.[48] He recommended that, in order to deal with tenants who failed to pay, the 'hanging gale' be maintained.[49] However, a more immediate problem was the task of breaking over 150 leases which had been granted by the previous Lord Digby. The leaseholders included descendants of substantial farmers, including a magistrate.[50] The leaseholders had built houses and had made significant improvements to the land they leased, resulting in what had been very marginal bogland being transformed into relatively productive land. They had improved their dwelling houses with 'every stick and stone of their own'.[51] Trench was convinced that the breaking of such leases would inevitably result in 'violence, bloodshed and murder'.[52] To solve the problem he proposed to go to England to negotiate with the executors of the late Lord Digby.

These were the plans Trench had for the Digby estate in 1857 but what were the local population's impressions of Trench and how did they react to his proposals to transform the district? Articles in local newspapers at the time suggest that the tenantry of Geashill were extremely worried and apprehensive about the impact of the 'new agent' on their lives and on the locality. Local parish priest, Father Kinsella, described how before Trench's arrival, 'Geashill was probably one of the most peaceful and orderly districts in the country under the agency of Mr John Digby; it had a happy and peaceful tenantry, with prosperity reigning in the midst of them, whereas after the arrival of Mr Trench and his son, the area became one of "armed assassins"'.[53] A letter to the editor of the *Nation* a few months after their appointment would suggest that both Trench and his son were somewhat uncomfortable in their new position and were concerned for their safety in Geashill. The castle was well fortified; both day and night a body of police was stationed there to guard it. 'Whenever Mr Trench senior and Mr Trench junior, appear ouside the castle's enclosure they are invariably accompanied by a brace of revolvers'. While the letter writer remarked that the barony was tranquil at the time he expressed a wish that it might continue that way. 'Would to Heaven, for their own sakes and for the sake of the poor entrusted to their tender mercies that so much could be said of the consciences of the two Trenches'![54]

2. Challenges of management at Geashill

Where an estate which has for a long time being neglected or 'let alone' and where the subdivision of land has been permitted to proceed unchecked, it will under ordinary circumstances take many years to remedy the evils, if indeed they can be ever remedied.[1]

It appears from this statement written by William Steuart Trench to Lord Digby in 1857 that the problem of subdivision was going to be one of the main challenges he would constantly face during his first year as manager on the estate. Trench acknowledged that this was a difficult issue for anyone engaged in the management of land.[2]

SUBDIVISION

Subdivision of land had been a major problem in Ireland from the beginning of the 19th century. As farms got smaller, tenants had less land to survive on, leading to widespread poverty, which was a contributory factor to the severe impact of the Great Famine in the 1840s. In the years after the Famine, the evils of subdivision still prevailed in many parts of Ireland. This practice was still very much a problem on the Digby estate up to the late 1850s. In fact, Trench considered subdivision as 'the most difficult to solve of any of the social problems in Ireland'. The total number of holdings on the Digby estate in 1857 was 889. Figure 4 illustrates the extent of the problem at Geashill where 102 holdings consisted of less than one acre of land and 170 holdings were below 10 acres. It is evident from the figures that large holdings were few and far between, with only one holding over 300 acres and only 11 holdings between 200 and 300 acres. Almost half the total number of tenants at Geashill were surviving on farms of under 10 acres. From the table it would appear that the majority of tenants survived by daily labour or by the cultivation of plots of ground that were so small in value and extent that it was impossible for the people to maintain themselves with a decent standard of living or comfort. Labour was very cheap in the district at the time, with labourers earning no more than 1s. per day.[3]

When reflecting on how to deal with the problem of overpopulation Trench considered measures introduced on other estates in Ireland where the problem was sternly dealt with, by 'making a clean sweep of the ancient

Holdings	Size of holding
102	Under one acre
41	Above 1 acre and not exceeding 2 acres
109	Above 2 acres and not exceeding 5 acres
128	Above 5 acres and not exceeding 10 acres
170	Above 10 acres and not exceeding 20 acres
112	Above 20 acres and not exceeding 30 acres
55	Above 30 acres and not exceeding 40 acres
35	Above 40 acres and not exceeding 50 acres
54	Above 50 acres and not exceeding 70 acres
40	Above 70 acres and not exceeding 100 acres
21	Above 100 acres and not exceeding 150 acres
10	Above 150 acres and not exceeding 200 acres
7	Above 200 acres and not exceeding 250 acres
4	Above 250 acres and not exceeding 300 acres
1	Above 300 acres

4 Classification of tenants' holdings on the Digby estate in 1857.
Source: 1857 Annual Report from Trench to Lord Digby

tenantry and replacing them with those from another country and another creed, whilst the old inhabitants have been forced to emigrate elsewhere'.[4] Such a 'sweeping system' would require vast expenditure and could militate against the landlord. Therefore, Trench recommended an alternative system, which involved Lord Digby taking directly under his control all the land previously held by middlemen. The only exception to this was the land of a few labourers, which continued under the control of large farmers. Trench considered this policy of land management a better system in the long run, making the point to Lord Digby that 'your lordship's rental will contain a greater number on the roll, than if middlemen had full power over the estate' and that 'no estate can ever preserve a wholesome constitution when crowded by miserable tenants, disowned by the lord of the soil and handed over to the mercies of local petty tyrants'.[5] He concluded by remarking that as soon as the landlord is directly responsible for these people, 'the evils of subdivision will appear in stronger colours'.[6] One would wonder if Trench had the tenants' best interests at heart or if it was an attempt to clear the estate of the less desirable members of the community and so lessen the power of middlemen who could have posed a threat to his management.

His long-term solution to subdivision would suggest that the latter was true. His solution was a policy of consolidation, which involved removing what he considered the 'worst characters' and adding their land to the farms of those who had proved themselves to be the 'best and most improving tenants'.[7] He had implemented this scheme on the Lansdowne estate in Kenmare and had succeeded in reducing the number of tenants on the estate there in a short time from 1,800 to 1,100. He carried out similar policies on the Bath estate in Co. Monaghan and by degrees he had greatly reduced the number of tenants there too. He made the point that the system in both cases cost the respective landlords a large sum of money as thousands emigrated through assisted emigration schemes. Many were bought out, while others left of their own accord. Trench considered this system a better, kinder and cheaper system than forced eviction, although he was aware that many of the tenants at Geashill may not have seen the situation that way. As Trench himself put it to Lord Digby, 'But let not your lordship vainly suppose that this system may satisfy the people, far from it, they would almost submit better to a severe and uncompromising ejectment'.[8]

He blamed much of the situation at Geashill on the 'mismanagement' by his predecessors, criticizing them for being overly considerate towards the tenants by maintaining them on the estate. He considered as kinder the landlords who, during the Famine, enabled people to emigrate, as they relieved their own estates of a 'crushing and disgraceful weight of pauperism, which is now infinitely more difficult to deal with'.[9] He made the point that very few people from the Geashill area ended up in the union workhouse either during the Great Famine or in the decade after it. In 1849, when many workhouses were full to the brim, only 136 people from the barony of Geashill were housed in the Tullamore workhouse. This was exceptionally low given the fact that the population on the estate at the time was 6,192.[10] The number of paupers attending the workhouse from the barony continued to decrease in the 1850s. In June, 1856 only 43 people from the barony were receiving union relief.[11] This low number was attributed to the little huts and freeholds located around the estate, which provided accommodation for those who might have been in the workhouse but were obviously sustained by the efforts made by both the previous landlords and agents to support the poor, independently of the poor house, partly by labour and partly by soup kitchens. While this system was well intentioned at the time, Trench considered the remnants of the system as an obstacle to his management plans for the estate, as it left behind a vast number of paupers who still lived in miserable huts on the road side or on the corners of fields 'paying no rent, having no visible means of a living, but who still adhere with a tenacity that is inconceivable to their miserable and half ruined cabins'.[12] He considered it would have been better for him and for the condition of the estate had these people entered the workhouse and been fed and remained there until their relatives sent for them to go to America. 'I fear they will prove a fruitful source of difficulty, annoyance and perhaps of danger to the system now about to be pursued'.[13] In this light, one must consider Trench's plans for the estate and the implications of these plans for the poorer sectors of the community at Geashill.

ARREARS

The Trenches soon came to realize that many tenants on the estate were in arrears. Some of them owed 3, 5, 10 and even 12 years rent. Most of these tenants were unable to pay such amounts. The arrears were owed to the previous landlord who had exceeded his powers by granting leases for lives and periods beyond his own life. When the late earl died, the new Lord Edward Digby was not entitled by law to collect any of these arrears since they belonged to the main line of the family that inherited the English estate and titles. Trench proposed to the new Lord Digby that he should buy the arrears owed from the executors at a sum much less than their full worth. The arrears would thus be owed to him and he would be entitled to collect them. Trench felt this was necessary since if the debts continued in the hands of the executors he was sure that they would never be collected and that any attempt to do so would result not only in large-scale resistance, but in the long term tenants might refuse the repayment of all rent. In 1857, the total arrears due were £40,948 17s. 4d. By July 1858, £7,074 10s. 1d. had been collected. £162 8s. 3d. was abandoned by Mr Thompson leaving a balance £33,711 19s. Trench blamed the accumulation of arrears on the inefficient management of his predecessors. It seemed that Thompson, the previous agent, had inherited a large sum of arrears and made little or no effort to collect it. In fact he had allowed it to increase by over £2,200.

    In an attempt to solve this problem at Geashill Lord Digby bought the arrears from the executors. However, some of the amount owed would be abandoned. Trench recommended that 50 per cent be struck off all arrears at once, this being an attempt to recognize the tenants who were reliable and always paid their rent. After deliberation with Lord Digby it was arranged that 'those leaseholders in arrears should be required to pay the remainder of their arrears in full out of money allowed them as compensation for their several leases and that they would then be reinstated on the estate as yearly tenants'.[14] Secondly, that yearly tenants in arrears who had shown some signs of improvements would be offered a 75 per cent reduction on the arrears on condition that they paid the 25 per cent balance in full. However, this arrangement did not suit a large number of tenants on the estate, especially those who according to Trench were in the habit of paying no rent at all. In dealing with the problem of arrears Trench almost created a new ethos at Geashill, given the fact that such customs only existed on estates in Ulster at the time and tenants in the south were not guaranteed the three Fs of a fair rent, fixity of tenure and free sale, until they were introduced in the 1870 Land Act. Here, Trench displayed formidable management skills by rewarding those who had invested in improvements or those he called solvent and upright tenants while he demanded prompt and full payment from the other tenants on the estate. Those who failed to meet his demands faced possible removal or eviction. Those forced from the estate left behind unpaid arrears. In the annual reports to Lord Digby these insolvent arrears are recorded as abandoned. In estimating the fixed voluntary charges for the estate, he included an annual sum of £500 for abandoned arrears, and another £500 for emigration and compensation.[15] By using this strategy to solve the problem of arrears on the estate, Trench succeeded in removing the smaller tenant farmers and paupers from Lord Digby's estate. This would greatly facilitate his plans for consolidation and improvements at Geashill. In the second annual report to Lord Digby, when examining the issue of payment of arrears, Trench stated, 'It is impossible to say how much of this will be paid; probably very little as it is chiefly due by paupers and Ribbonmen, both of whom it would be most desirable to rid the estate'.[16]

LEASE-BREAKING

A more immediate problem facing Trench on taking up his appointment was that of lease breaking. He was given the task of breaking 158 leases. The leaseholders had built houses and had made significant improvements to the land they leased, resulting in what had been very marginal bog land being transformed into relatively productive land. They had improved their dwelling at their own cost or as previously stated 'with every stick and stone of their own'.[17] Some cottiers were employed by leaseholders who gave them small plots of land; others squatted on the land and felt they had a right to it. On hearing of the lease-breaking that was to take place, the tenants held meetings where they deliberated, before appealing to the landlord and to the executors of the late peer. 'Pending the ejectment procedures they were passed from "post to pillar" without any satisfaction'.[18] Convinced that the breaking of such leases would inevitably result in violence and bloodshed,[19] Trench's fears were soon confirmed when police informed him of a threat to kill Lord Digby, 'a bloody death awaited him if he pressed matters to issue with his tenants'.[20]

Armed with this news and a statement of the notary valuation made by the surveyors Brassington and Gale of all the leaseholders, totalling £30,628,[21] Trench went to London to negotiate with the executors of the late Lord Edward Digby. According to the 1858 annual report George Wingfield Digby had previously agreed to compensate tenants for the breaking of leases. He

felt he was bound as a man of honour to make compensation to the
leaseholders on the Geashill estate for the loss of sundry leases illegally granted
to them by the late earl and which the new Lord Digby wished to break. The
new landlord instructed Trench to confer with Mr Richard Wingfield Digby,
brother of George, who inherited the late earl's English property, on the
amount to be given and the mode of distribution. He met with the executors
of the late landlord and presented Brassington and Gale's valuation, which
amounted to £30,628.[22] This evaluation was slightly above the official Griffith's
valuation.[23] He proposed on Lord Digby's behalf 'that the sum be paid at once
to his lordship'.[24] In chapter 20 of *Realities of Irish life*, Trench portrays himself
as 'an honest broker' acting on behalf of the tenants:

> I endeavoured to prove to them in the first place, that claims of the
> tenantry for compensation for the loss of their leases were just and fair,
> and might perhaps on trial be proved to be legal also and in the second
> place, I assured them if they yielded the principle of compensation, no
> unreasonable demands would be made.[25]

Soon after his appointment Trench visited all the leaseholders, as he had
presumed that their dwellings would have shown signs of improvement.
However, he pointed out that the holdings in the worst condition were those
in the hands of leaseholders. He acknowledged that some farms he visited had
visible signs of improvement but unfortunately these were in the minority and,
in general, the tenants at will had carried out as many improvements as the
leaseholders had. The leaseholders who did show evidence of improvements
included tenants such as Richard Odlum of Ballyduff South, John Tarleton of
Killeigh, Mr Delamere of Meelaghans while the most improving tenants at
will were Mr Odlum of Cappincur, John Rigney of Meelaghans, A. Flanagan
of Cappincur and Mr Todd of Cappanageeragh.

Trench argued that the leaseholders were entitled to compensation,
although they had done little to improve their land, while tenants at will were
entitled to no compensation, even if improvements had been carried out. After
much debate, Trench secured the total amount on condition that 'his lordship
would undertake to protect the executors and defend any lawsuits at his own
cost which might be commenced against them for any further compensation
or claim'.[26] This would also free George Wingfield Digby from any blame or
possible lawsuits against him for lease breaking. The money was lodged in
Tullamore Bank to the joint credit of Lord Digby and Trench.[27] Trench
proposed to compensate tenants by offering them the amount, or nearly the
amount, awarded by Brassington and Gale, but this money would only be
offered to leaseholds which he considered 'entire' and not to those subdivided
or underlet. In cases where subdivision or underletting had taken place he

proposed to reserve a proportional sum to be given as compensation for the removal, or remuneration, of those he proposed to dispose of.

On his return, Trench feared that negotiations with the tenants might not go as smoothly. To avoid further confrontation and a possible lawsuit, his strategy was to divide and conquer, and consequently he called ten of the most extensive and those whom he considered the most 'respectable'[28] tenants together. In his 1858 report to Lord Digby, Trench summed up the initial attitude of those leading tenants by saying, 'some were secretly anxious for law, others thought the sum offered to be insufficient, a few thought it fair, while others distrusted the whole affair and refused to sign'.[29] He concluded by saying that by degrees all difficulties were overcome and the tenants agreed to his terms. In dealing with lease-breaking did Trench display conciliatory tactics or did he pressurize the tenants into agreeing to his terms? His tactic here was to wait until the last day on which it was possible to hold a conference, before a pending lawsuit commenced. At this meeting he persuaded the tenants to accept his terms there and then. It appears that a few of the leading tenants were not happy with the deal on offer and put up some resistance to signing the consent form. One Mr Warren was offered £1,200 but demanded £1,400, Trench gave him £1,300. Mr Conroy was also dissatisfied with the sum on offer, while Richard Odlum only agreed to sign on condition that he was guaranteed to be retained as a tenant on the estate. Trench could not promise this and it seemed that Odlum was reduced to tears.[30] However, it seems that the one who put up the most resistance was Mr Flanagan of Cappincur, who wanted to deliberate and consult other tenants before signing. According to Trench, 'Flanagan was very disagreeable in his manner and tried to pervert many things I said and I had to sharply correct him on the spot'.[31] Trench insisted that Flanagan sign there and then, 'if you delay, the English witnesses will be over, we shall then take a different course altogether, and it will be up to you to say if you will be so liberally dealt with'.[32] It is therefore reasonable to conclude that Trench bullied or pressurized Flanagan and others to agreeing to his terms: 'you must come to a decision now; there is a messenger at the door on horseback, to ride to the telegraph station at Portarlington to stop the English witnesses from coming over, this must be done within an hour'.[33] One by one they accepted his terms and the other tenants followed suit. In fact, out of 158 leaseholders, 146 signed. There were certain individual cases, where Lord Digby dealt himself with the tenants, although it is not clear what the circumstances were. All tenants who agreed signed compensation vouchers and received cheques for the agreed sum.

A common tactic employed by Trench when dealing with subdivision, lease-breaking and arrears, was an attempt to rid the estate of the poorer sectors of the community. How did the tenants react to the new type of management on the Digby estate? A letter to the *Leinster Journal*, dated 28 January 1858, titled the 'Two Trenches' gave the following description of Geashill a few months after the appointment of the new agents: 'operations have been commenced by smashing every lease made by the late kind hearted proprietor'. The article went on to say that the next step was to raise the rents and 'that now every tenant on this vast estate is required under *penalty of expulsion*, to put his name to a paper of *rules and regulations* of the most odious, grinding and tyrannical character'. This article suggested that the Trenches were somewhat uncomfortable in their new position, 'public report has it, that they feel this position in Geashill a very uncomfortable one'. It also suggested that they may not be safe in their new abode. It stated that 'day and night a body of police are stationed there to guard it from all manner of assault'. The author who signed himself 'B' ended by acknowledging that the barony was peaceful and tranquil at present and expressed a wish that it would remain so.[34]

RIBBONISM

It seemed that the actions of the two Trenches swiftly led the tenants at Geashill to turn to societies such as the 'Ribbonmen'. This was an illegal Catholic association set up in 1808.[35] The society originated from previous secret societies such as the Defenders, who were themselves largely subsumed into the Society of the United Irishmen in 1798.[36] The name is derived from a green ribbon worn as a badge in a button-hole by the members. The society was formed in response to the miserable conditions in which the tenant farmers and labourers lived and worked in the early 19th century. Depending on the district, the society was variously known as the Fraternal Society, the Patriotic Association or the Sons of the Shamrock. The main aims of this society were, first, to prevent any landlord, under any circumstance whatever, from depriving any tenant of his land and, secondly, to deter, 'on pain, of almost certain death'[37] any tenant from taking land from which any other tenant was evicted. Their actions were carried out with great severity and aimed at wealthy landlords and humble cottiers alike. At a local level, Ribbonism operated as a parish or district lodge, composed of around 30 members, their usual meeting place being the public house. The main meeting place for the local Ribbonmen in Geashill was a pub at Cross Keys near the village. The increase in Ribbon activity in the barony coincided with the arrival of both Trench and his son on Lord Digby's estate. In fact the Trenches were so unpopular and hated by many that members of the local Ribbon Society began to devise a method of getting rid of Trench. As Trench himself noted 'conspiracies for various subscriptions were set on foot to pay for the murder of myself and my son'.[38]

William Trench and his son were to be made aware of this fact by informers or as he put it himself 'secret friends'. It is said that an agent had a hundred eyes and a hundred ears.[39] Godkin attributed many of Mr Trench's victories over his tenants on the Geashill estate to the spy network he had created. He suggested that many tenants who turned up to the estate office seeking favours found it useful to spy on their neighbours.[40] Trench's use of spies was not unique to Geashill but rather a common tactic employed by the Trenches in their management strategy on both their Monaghan and Kerry estates, where they used a system of 'local espionage'. One of his chief informants in Geashill was a young girl originally from Kenmare who then lived in an area of the estate described as an area of ill repute.[41] Her name was Mary Shea and she worked as a maid in a public house where the Ribbonmen constantly met, at Cross Keys.[42] She indicated to the police that she had information on ribbon activity in the district but would only be willing to tell it to Mr Trench's other son, Thomas Townsend, who worked in Kenmare. William Trench was obviously anxious for the information, since his son from Kenmare was summoned to Geashill. Perhaps one should question what kind of a relationship and past she had had with Townsend Trench and why she was living in Geashill in the first place.

Ribbon activity had increased and seemed rife in the district in 1860. This coincided with Trench's new style of management and was a direct response to his consolidation policies, his breaking of leases and his dealing with the problems of arrears, all of which impinged on the poorer sectors of the community. In fact while some incidents were labelled as 'Ribbon Activity' they were really the reactions of aggrieved tenants to his management. A woodman, named Harvey, an employee of Trench, had been attacked in his house by a number of armed men and it was Trench's belief that this was done to intimidate anyone who attempted to carry out the new rules of the estate.[43] Another event that excited much interest in the county was when Henry Kane of Killurin refused to give up possession of his brother's land, which he had occupied on his brother's death. Large crowds gathered around his house to sympathize with him. He was cheered and supported by the dispossessed and subscriptions were raised to enable him to defend the ejection. Trench recommended to Lord Digby that this man should be put off the estate and be made an example of.[44] However, it seemed that the Kane case was only one of many, as Trench informed Lord Digby that 'numerous letters were sent around the barony so that scarcely a servant could be hired or a shepherd discharged, without ribbon notices flying about all concerned'.[45] Other cases included that which occurred at Annagharvey, where a large body of men surrounded the house and set fire to a hayrick of a Mrs Pattison, described by Trench as a respectable Protestant tenant.

Trench was also made aware that money was being collected for the assassination of himself and his son.[46] In fact, such was his concern for his safety that he had all the window shutters in the lower part of his house doubled and made more secure.[47] In 1858, Nassau Senior who visited King's County, recalled how Trench informed him that he never went out without arms, or without being attended by two armed men.[48] Not only did the Trenches fear for their lives but so also did many of the new leaseholders who had taken over land previously held by another tenant. Hugh Nesbitt, the local baliff who had replaced a James Lawrence as a leaseholder in the townland of Ballydownan wrote to Thomas Trench in February 1860, expressing his concerns for his safety and informed Trench that he had to have all his windows sheeted with iron.[49] In the same correspondence he told how Patrick Murphy, the blacksmith from Newtown had informed him that Darby Flanagan had £120 collected for the shooting of Thomas Weldon Trench. He stated that he was also aware that a William Malone of Danganbeg was asked for money for the same cause, by Loughlin Kelly and John Whelaghan, two of the other ring leaders.[50] Nesbitt also informed Mr Trench that two tenants who had taken over farms in Rathfeston on a Mr Pimm's property had received threatening notices.[51]

While Trench had taken a somewhat passive role towards Ribbon activity in the first three years of his management, the increased activities of the organization were to cause a change in tactic. He planned to take legal steps to rid the estate of Ribbonmen. The services of Mary Shea, his spy at Cross Keys, was to play a major role in obtaining the vital information needed for him to execute his plans and his son Thomas Townsend Trench was to be instrumental in the gathering of this information. In a letter written by Townsend to his father, dated 10 February 1860, he gave a clear account of his visit to Miss Shea and of the vital information. He began the letter by stating, 'I have had a very full and interesting interview of from 3 to 4 hours with the young woman who seemed so anxious to confide the depths of her soul into young hands certainly the atmosphere here is impregnated with war in a curious manner'.[52] As previously stated one must question how well this girl was known to Mr Trench Junior. In fact, when he addressed her by saying, 'sure I saw you before Mary, eh!' She replied by saying 'Oh bedad I often seen you Sir!'[53] When describing the Ribbonmen in the barony she said they are the worst she has ever seen, 'They'd take your life for a glass of whiskey while they'd be looking at you'.[54] She named a Loughlin Kelly and Whelaghan as two of the ring leaders and told how she overheard them one night in the pub plotting to murder his brother and father. Other leaders named were Flanagan, Healion and Johnny Clibburn. She detailed their various activities in the district informing Trench that she would be willing to testify. It seemed that Mr Trench Senior soon acted on this information and in his 1860 report to Lord Digby told how a notice to quit had been served on a man called Loughlin Kelly who was known to be 'the worse character and treasurer of the murder fund'.[55] He was ejected and, much to the dismay of the barony, he was put out on the road by the sheriff accompanied by 25 policemen to preserve the peace. His house and 60 acres were subsequently handed to Trench. Such action was followed by the serving of notices to quit on four or five other leading Ribbonmen, to be followed by legal proceedings against them. After a visit by Trench to Healion there was an attempt made to burn Trench's residence. In fact the offices at Geashill castle were destroyed and had to be rebuilt. Trench became increasingly concerned for his safety and therefore a policeman was assigned to give protection to him and his son. However, this may well have been a ploy by Trench to eliminate one of the Ribbon leaders from the district. By attributing the blame for the fire at the castle to Healion, Trench was quick to ascribe any opposition to conspiracy with local Ribbonmen which further facilitated his plans for 'clearance' of the estate. Other sources suggest that the castle fire was in fact caused by some of Trench's own servants.[56] In his memoir *Realities of Irish life* Trench implied that after the elimination of the leading Ribbonmen from the estate, peace prevailed. Correspondence and later reports to Lord Digby would suggest that the crisis was escalating though, and that Ribbonism was alive and well in Geashill up to the 1870s. In fact, he admitted that 'the notice to quit on Ribbonmen and the eviction of Loughlin Kelly and Healion seem to be bringing maters to a crisis'.[57] In 1862, a Mr Denning, a Protestant who was manager of the Bank of Ireland in Tullamore, reported to Trench that a sub-inspector of the constabulary informed him of plans to attack him for taking over land. He said that he feared for some of his labourers.[58] He ended the correspondence by informing Trench that one of his sheep had died the previous Saturday night 'under very extraordinary circumstances'.[59] It seemed that Mr Denning was prevented from adding a piece of land to his property due to his fear of Ribbonmen.[60] In 1864, a number of outrages in the barony caused by Ribbon activity, including a number of burglaries, were reported to Lord Digby.[61] Apparently, the police did not act against the Ribbonmen, indeed Trench referred to them as 'ineffective' and said that 'the people were taking matters into their own hands'.[62] Perhaps the police also feared for their lives as in 1868 the police barracks had to be fortified with protection mechanisms such as iron doors and windows and loop-holes.[63] It is therefore reasonable to conclude that the first few years of Trench's agency may have seen him successfully break leases, end subdivision and solve the problem of arrears, however, these years were also characterized by a wave of discontent among the tenantry which proved to be a more controversial aspect of his management of the Digby estate.

3. Improvements at Geashill

While the first few years of Trench's management of the estate at Geashill was characterized by conflict, conspiracies, threats and evictions, the latter part of his time there saw advancements and improvements. Would this alter the legacy of Trench's agency? Would he be remembered as the tyrant who broke leases, evicted tenants and as a result feared for his life from Ribbonmen who sought revenge, or would his legacy be one of the improver who was well ahead of his time? Or can improvements carried out on the Digby estate between 1857 and 1872 be attributed to the new landlord, Edward St Vincent Digby? Whatever the answer to these questions, the years of Trench's agency in Geashill were to prove to be significant in the history of the barony and one that left a lasting imprint on the landscape.

The village of Geashill was practically rebuilt after 1860, the old thatched cottages were replaced with stone ones with slated roofs and several drainage schemes were implemented to enhance the quality of the land. In fact much of the present form of what is now Geashill and its surrounding areas owes its origin to the work carried out in the 1860s. But what was the physical condition of the barony in the early part of the 19th century and what topographical and structural challenges faced Trench in his management of Lord Digby's estate? It is clear from the topographical and statistical survey of Sir Charle Coote carried out as early as 1801 that the tenants on the Digby estate were totally dependent on agriculture. In fact Coote said that 'every acre of this barony being the estate of Viscount Digby is almost entirely inhabited by farmers'.[1] The size of the fields were between 5 and 15 acres, were irregular in shape and consisted of wet bog and moorland. Few attempts were made to reclaim any ground. Crops grown included wheat, oats, barley, potatoes and rape seed, while black cattle and sheep were reared there. Geashill was particularly distinguished for having the best pig fair in the province of Leinster, if not in the entire country. It was frequented by buyers from Cork, Waterford and other provincial towns.[2] The estate had much potential, having access to four markets at Tullamore, Mountmellick, Phillipstown and Portarlington, a demand for hay to feed the horses of the soldiers of the nearby garrison towns and the availability of a brewery and a distillery at Tullamore which required the raw materials of barley and oats. However, there was very little incentive for the tenants to improve the land, as leases did not exceed 21 years and farming methods were antiquated and backward. The living conditions of the tenants were just as bad with the majority of them living in mud cabins along the roadside or in marginal areas of bog. Did conditions improve with Ireland's progression into the 19th century? Samuel Lewis, when giving a geographical description of Geashill in 1837, described the soil as deep clay, with a large extent of bogland. He suggested that agriculture was poor and little improved.[3] According to Richard Griffith's valuation of the early 1850s there were extensive tracts of bogland over much of the barony.[4] One can therefore conclude that few, if any, attempts were made to improve either the quality of the land or the living conditions of the tenants on the Digby estate in the early part of the 19th century. Trench's own account of events concurred with this when he described the condition of the estate in 1857 as one of the most wretched he had seen.

During the 1840s Ireland had lost 282,000 houses and the number declined further in the 1850s and 1860s.[5] Most of the houses consisted of cabins of the poorest classes in society, usually located in marginal areas in a dispersed pattern. The barony of Geashill was no exception to this. The dwellings of the farmers were in poor condition, most consisting of thatch and mud. The houses of some of the poorer classes remained situated on the periphery of the bog. Bog fires were common and when they occurred many of the poor lost their entire home and any crops they had in storage were also destroyed. While emigration was one solution to much of Ireland's run-down landscape in the middle of the 19th century, Trench noted that in Geashill there was no desire on the tenants' part to leave the estate and in his 1862 report to Lord Digby commented that 'the desire of the tenants to hold on to their farms is so striking that it forms one of the main difficulties in our management'.[6]

The Trenches embarked upon a regeneration project. This saw most of the mud hovels being replaced with stone and mortar houses, which were well built, roofed with slate and timber, while existing cottages were improved by the addition of windows and chimneys. This had the advantage of providing much stronger and sturdier dwellings with much needed light and fresh air while at the same time enabling the tenants to put their straw on the manure instead of being used as thatch. In fact much of the present layout and structure of Geashill village emerged at this time. The cottages located on the left-hand side on the approach road from Portarlington owe their origin to the Trench project. Throughout the 1860s Trench, on behalf of Lord Edward St Vincent Digby, embarked upon a major project of house improvement, not only in the village of Geashill but throughout the entire barony. As early as 1862, only five years into Trench's agency, there is evidence of minor works and repairs to 106 tenants' houses and this had greatly enhanced the condition and appearance of the district. While a great number of new houses were constructed between 1857 and 1872, for example, new treble cottages were built in the village in 1861 at a cost of £103 3s. 3d. and single cottages for £77 16s. 5d.,[7] Trench thought it more profitable and less expensive to improve existing dwellings.

Houses of W. Coogan
and P. Byrne in 1857
(*above*) and in 1861
(*below*).

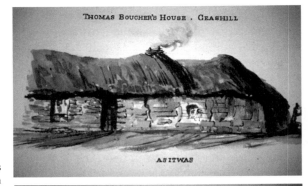

Thomas Boucher's
House Geashill in
1857 (*above*) and in
1861 (*below*).

5 Cottages before and after renovation. *Source:* Digby private collection, Dorset.

Eliza'Ennis's House Curragh, Geashill, 1857 (*above*) and in 1861 (*below*).

Joseph Mulpeter's House, Ballydownan, Geashill, 1857 (*above*) and in 1861 (*below*).

In fact he reported to Lord Digby in 1869 how he saw 'ten good wholesome dwellings made out of ten wretched old houses at the price that would have only built five new dwellings'.[8] The cost was £9 per dwelling.[9] It seemed that improvements continued to be carried out to the buildings on the Digby estate throughout the 1860s and into the 1870s. In the year 1871 alone, the total spent by Lord Digby on new buildings was £462 2s. 6d. and this included the construction of some wooden cottages. However, repairs amounted to £1066 11s. 11d. which included the remodelling of old houses.[10]

The success of such schemes of house building and repairs not only enhanced the appearance of the barony and improved the living conditions of the tenants but it also earned Lord Digby recognition both at home and abroad. His schemes proved so successful that the Digby estate won the gold medal offered by the Royal Agricultural Society of Ireland for the best labourers' cottages in the province of Leinster.[11] The estate also boasted of holding the duke of Leinster challenge cup for the best labourers' cottages in Ireland for three successive years. At a meeting of the Royal Agricultural Society of Ireland held in Sackville Street, in May 1865, the plans of a number of labourer's cottages on the Digby estate were submitted for competition by William Trench. The subsequent report said that the:

> cottages were well built and finished; they are all on the ground floor and consist of a good kitchen and two good bedrooms. They are well flagged with a strong grit of sandstone flag, admirably suited cottage floors, as it is warm, dry, and of sufficient thickness to bear the hard usage of a labourer's cottage; will wash well and does not appear to flake off, as some sandstones do. We particularly wish to direct attention to the way in which every recess was made available, either by shelves, cupboards, or boxes for the use and convenience of the inhabitants.[12]

Lord Digby was thus awarded the gold medal for the province of Leinster for six well-finished cottages which were deemed the most comfortable in which to live. He was also successful at an international level when in 1867 he was awarded a bronze medal for cottages at the Paris Exhibition.[13]

Sketches of cottages on the Digby estate in 1857 and in 1861 survive and illustrate that the improvements carried out in a four-year period were remarkable: thatched roofs were replaced with slate and timber, walls were constructed with stone and mortar and each house had more and better windows (figure 5). Overall, the cost of expenditure on buildings and repairs was £14,056.[14] However Trench admitted that £3,362 was given to tenants for surrender of tenements. This suggests that he may have been somewhat selective in the class of tenant who experienced improvements to their holdings. When examining the census returns for Geashill during Trench's agency, one can conclude that the number of houses had declined by 515.[15] The annual reports show that in 1862 alone, 142 houses were levelled, probably as part of the improvement schemes.[16] While a significant number of tenants at Geashill experienced considerable improvements to their dwellings and which earned Lord Digby both national and international acclaim, the 1861 report from William Trench to the landlord revealed that £280 3s. consisting chiefly of small sums were given to enable those who surrendered their holdings to find a means of livelihood elsewhere.[17] The same report reveals that a sum of £132 8s. 4d. had enabled 52 people to leave the estate.[18] This, together with the census returns of the period, displayed a 34.9 per cent decrease in the number of houses and percentage decline of 40.3 per cent in the population of the barony between 1851 and 1871.[19] This suggests that in order to make way for improvements carried out on the Digby estate in the 1860s, Trench cleared parts of the estate by knocking down houses and removing tenants. Therefore, not all tenants in the barony of Geashill were to share in the improvements of the Trench years.

Selective or not, the years 1857–71 resulted in massive improvements to the houses throughout the barony. While these changes were evident throughout the 30,000 acre estate, the village of Geashill also underwent a major transformation. Not only were the homes of labourers enhanced but the 1860s saw the erection of a new national school, estate office and workshop, renovations to the castle as well as the completion of a new road which linked Geashill to Tullamore and the remodelling of the village inn. As early as 1858 Trench saw the need for a new national school. He made an agreement with the commissioners of national education to build a new school house in the village. Under this agreement, Lord Digby provided a free site across from the church and promised to pay one third of the cost, while the commissioners would pay the remaining two-thirds. The school was completed in 1862. In the 1863 annual report to Lord Digby, Trench described the new school house as 'a building which for permanence of structure and elegance of design and execution is we believe, in the school line, admitted to be unrivalled in Ireland'.[20] Many photographs of this new building are contained in the Digby private collection.[21] Perhaps Trench had a point as the original building is still well preserved and continues to be part of the present day national school in the village.

It seems that the Digby family took a great interest in the new school and made generous donations and gave gifts to it, as is evident from the many letters written from the staff to Lady Digby. One such letter was written by a Michael Mulpeter to Lady Digby dated August 1870, thanked her for her generous gift of a book. The school had a substantial number on the roll book. In 1869 it had a total of 70 students, while 25 children attended the Church of Ireland school.[22] In 1870, 69 students were on the roll of the new school

6 The new school at Geashill, opened in 1862

while the number of children attending the Protestant school had increased
to 31.[23]

In the same year as the completion of the school, a new estate office (now
the Garda Station in the village) was constructed, located beside the church
and next to the castle. A lock-up area, new stables and a shed for carts were
added to the castle grounds.[24] The castle itself also underwent renovations.
When Trench arrived in the village the roof of the castle was leaking and there
was a need for two new water closets with corresponding sewers.[25] By 1861
the old ballroom and what were described as two indifferent rooms were
converted into an excellent parlour, drawing room, two good bedrooms and
a dressing room.[26] In 1862 the barracks was fortified with loop holes and iron
windows capable of resisting attack.[27] This however was probably more of a
necessity than a desire for improvement, as Trench said that it enabled 'men to
hold their own until assistance arrived'[28] indicating that despite such vast
improvements all was not peaceful in the barony. 1868 saw the construction
of a carpenter's workshop in the village. This was located beside the architect's
house and a tenant agreed to surrender his house and offices on moderate
terms to allow this development. For ten years prior to this, carpenters had to
work in a low cowshed without windows and with very little light. The old
house was cleaned out, the walls raised and the roof slated. This became a
carpenter's shop while the old offices were converted to an 80 ft long store

room. The architect at the time, a Mr Masterson, was sent to London to examine the structure and composition of buildings there. It was decided to use local gravel and stone from the nearby Esker Hill's quarry to construct the workshop and a number of other projects being undertaken simultaneously, namely an excellent house for a Mr Delamere, which cost £290 and a new dwelling house adjoining the mill for a Mr Casey.[29]

One of Trench's priorities in the 1860s was to transform the land on the estate from one of infertility and bogland to good productive farmland. This was achieved through a series of land drainage schemes, consolidation of holdings and the implementation of improved farming techniques. He embarked upon a vigorous plan to drain an extensive area of wetland located between Geashill and Tullamore. In his memoir *Realities of Irish life* Trench described the land as consisting of 'wet moor' and as 'barren'.[30] Due to subdivision, the fields were very fragmented, so Trench realized he would have to 'lay out all the land anew',[31] in order to level the old fences, square and enlarge all the fields and sink deep drains, some of which resembled canals. In order to restore the land to full productivity, the land was levelled and planted with good quality grass seed to allow it to regain its nutrients. Trench had Peruvian guano applied to improve its fertility. This proved successful resulting in large-scale production of turnips, potatoes, wheat, oats and later, rape seed. In fact rape seed continues to be produced on this section of land up to the present. Although costly at the time, it seems that these schemes paid for themselves in the long run. Land which was previously let at a rent of 4s. per acre, now earned between 25 and 30s. per acre.[32] Over 100 acres of land in the townland of the Meelaghans were reclaimed and let to a Mr Marcus Goodbody, described by Trench as one of the richest men in Tullamore at the time.[33] Marcus was a member of the T.P. and R. Goodbody family who had a large tobacco factory in Tullamore and a jute factory in Clara in the 1860s. The newly reclaimed lands impressed a number of influential people, including Mr Frederick Denning, a banker in Tullamore, who after a visit to the estate was so impressed that he entered into a 21-year lease, and embarked upon an extensive system of similar reclamation.[34] Another successful scheme was carried out in the townlands of Ballina and Ballyknockan, described by Trench as 'formerly the most uncivilized and miserable spot on the estate, it is now one of the most highly cultivated and improved breadths of land on the property'.[35] Over 300 acres of swamp land were reclaimed. Fields were amalgamated and their boundaries straightened. A major drain over 12 feet deep was dug and a number of minor ones were placed at 30 feet intervals to facilitate surface run-off. Overall the cost was £2,424 18s. 8d.[36] In his annual report to Lord Digby, Trench said that he believed that 'this was a necessary cost and that it would transform one of the wildest districts of the estate into one of the most improved and cultivated'.[37] Another major drainage and

7 Layout of field patterns and house at Ballymooney, Geashill.
Source: cover page of 1868 Annual Report from Trench to Lord Digby

reclamation scheme was introduced in the townland of Ballincollin in 1862.
This involved the straightening, widening and deepening of 80 perches of the
Toberfin River, levelling 1,350 perches of useless fences and replacing them
with new sound ones. The plan, estimated to cost £1,114s. 12d. also included
clearing 127 acres of furze, the creation of 502 perches of ditches and the
building of new bridges.[38] Not only were schemes like this one successful at
restoring the land to full productivity but they also generated much needed
employment for labourers as 'there was not one unemployed hand in the
district'.[39] The quality, layout and appearance of the land were greatly improved
as an illustration, taken from the cover of the 1868 annual report to Lord Digby,
shows. Field patterns were larger and more regular in shape in 1868 which
would have facilitated a more intensive system of farming (figure 7).

By the end of the 1860s it seems that much of the land on the Digby estate
was transformed into good productive land and, as with his plan of cottage
design, such improvements in land drainage won Lord Digby national acclaim.
In 1869 the Royal Agricultural Society of Ireland awarded him the Gold Medal
and Hall Challenge Cup for the third time. The plan submitted, dated 12 July
1870, consists of reports, maps and costs of 64.25 acres of land submitted for
competition for the Gold Medal award offered by the society in 1869. The
submission consisted of four lots of land, lot number one consisted of 37.5
acres, located in the townland of Ballycollin, lot number two consisted of seven
acres located in the townland of Annagharvey. Lots three and four were located
in Ballyduff South and consisted of 11 and 9.75 acres respectively.[40] The work
was carried out by day labourers, under the supervision of Mr Henry Millie

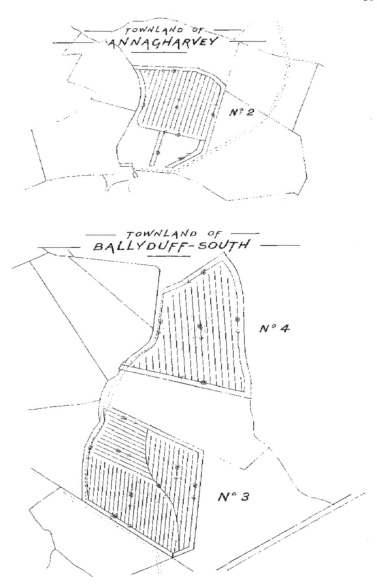

8 Part of the Drainage Plan submitted to the Royal Agricultural Society by Trench in 1869. *Source:* Offaly Historical and Archaeological Society's office, Tullamore

who was an experienced estate engineer and surveyor. He worked on the estate for over 30 years, extensively on drainage schemes undertaken on the estate in the 1860s and 1870s.[41] The labourers were paid 1s. 3d. a day and were provided with free home and garden. The land in lots one, two and three were drained with ditches four feet deep and 30 feet apart, while lot four consisted of deep bog necessitating the construction of drains four to five feet deep and 40 feet apart. This resulted in land being thoroughly dried.[42] The lots were also laid out in well organized and regular field patterns as can be seen from the drainage plans submitted. The total cost of the reclamation was £428 10s.[43] Having won the cup, valued at 50 guineas, for three years it then became the property of Lord Digby.[44] Anxious to encourage competition for good drainage in Ireland, he in turn presented a cup to the society, to be called the 'Digby Challenge Cup'.[45] In a letter to the society he wrote 'I shall be happy to present another of the same value, say fifty guineas, called the Digby Challenge Cup'.[46] This cup would be awarded to the candidate who succeeded in achieving the best drained lands for three successive years. This initiative demonstrates how, as an absentee landlord, Lord Digby was not only dedicated to improving his Geashill property but was also eager to encourage advancement on other Irish estates.

Land drainage continued to be an important part of Trench's management of Lord Digby's estate into the 1870s. To facilitate such drainage schemes a supply of permanent labourers was required. It seemed that Trench had difficulty in maintaining workers, as most of them were supplied by local farmers and only turned up when they were not needed on the farms. Thus he was often left without workers during the most important months of the year. It was suggested at the Paris Exhibition that he construct a moveable 'Russian village' to house his workers. Twelve timber cottages were constructed at Ballyknockan and Killeenmore with timber countersunk at the corners and laid one on top of the other, thus forming walls (figure 9). In this way, Trench secured a permanent well-trained workforce, who along with their cottages could be transported at a 'trifling cost to any district in which they may be required'.[47] The Russian village, like a modern day portakabin, enabled Trench to carry out work all year round with a steady supply of men. This proved successful and he reported that:

> the Russian village has enabled us to carry on the works with a steady and trained gang of men all year round and the houses seem to be highly approved of by their inhabitants. They are now working at thorough drainage in Newtown, which we hope will soon be finished and will complete the reclamation of a large tract of land which for some years has produced no rent, being thoroughly wet and useless.

9 Drawing of Russian Cottage erected as a portakabin for labourers.
Source: Digby Private Collection

Given the extent of drainage projects carried out, the cost of this 'moveable village', £144 19*s*., seemed a worthwhile investment and it displayed Trench's desire to adopt new ideas, allowing him to continue his work uninterrupted. The 1870 annual report shows that £769 2*s*. 6*d*. was spent on thorough drainage and £522 3*s*. 3*d*. on main drainage. The area concentrated on consisted of 45 acres located between the railway and the Tullamore road and Newtown. This resulted in the fields being squared and well fenced with large drains. The quality of land opposite the Russian houses was also improved by the addition of Dublin dairy manure. It would seem that such schemes were successful, as Trench reported that all this land was re-let to the adjoining tenants at a considerably higher rent. While the previous rent earned for many years was 5*s*. per Irish acre, the rent for the improved land was 40*s*. per Irish acre.[48] Lands previously considered pools of water now produced good crops of potatoes and land in Ballinagar that had previously lain in permanent water where cattle were in constant danger of drowning were now areas of good pasture.[49] Overall, the tenants seemed to have appreciated the improved drainage carried out on the estate and were willing to pay the increased rent. In 1871 Trench reported to Lord Digby that

A marked improvement is visible to the most casual observer not only in the houses of the tenantry but also in the habits of the people and in the tillage and agriculture of the district. Green crops, which some years ago were almost unknown among the greater portion of the tenantry are now very general. The land is better cultivated, better pasture prevails and the improvements in the breed of cattle has been considerable.[50]

While Trench has been credited with the implementation of similar improvements on the Lansdowne estate in Co. Kerry and in particular to the town of Kenmare, one must question if such improvements were instigated by Trench or if he was merely the instrument used to carry out the wishes of his employers? When assessing his time in Geashill, it was perhaps no coincidence that the estate underwent a major transformation as Lord Edward Digby, the then landlord was the grandson of Thomas Coke, first earl of Leicester, who was not only a British politician but a noted agricultural reformer. Coke became famous for his advanced methods of animal husbandry used in improving his estate at Holkham in Norfolk. As a result he was seen as one of the instigators of the British agricultural revolution. It therefore seems very likely that, like his grandfather, Edward St Vincent Digby was the instigator of the improvements carried out at Geashill during the 1860s.

4. Realities for the tenantry

Did the agency of William Steuart Trench alter the population trends on the Digby estate? An examination of the 1851 and 1871 census suggests that the population totals and distribution altered significantly during the two decades. In fact, the total population declined from 6,221, in 1851 to 3,712 in 1871, a percentage decline of 40.3 per cent for the period.

The number of houses also declined in the same period by 34.9 per cent. The full impact of these improvement schemes is best answered by examining the results of Trench's policies on a small number of townlands within the barony. As previously stated, in 1869 the Royal Agricultural Society of Ireland awarded Lord Digby the Gold Medal and Hall Challenge Cup for the third time for improvements to the townlands of Annagharvey, Ballycollin and Ballyduff South. Although not included in the competition the townland of Ballinvalley also experienced considerable improvements in reclamation. These improvements altered both the housing and population totals in all four townlands.

Eleven houses disappeared from Annagharvey, three from Ballycollin and eight from Ballyduff South, while the number of houses in the townland of Ballinvalley decreased from 68 in 1851 to 44 in 1871.[1] Statistics for the population totals in the corresponding townlands also show a decrease of 42 people in Annagharvey, 18 in Ballycollin, 50 Ballyduff South and 98 Ballinvalley. It is therefore reasonable to conclude that Trench felt the process of clearance and 'weeding out' was a necessary requisite to estate improvement.

While Trench was noted for his assisted emigration schemes in counties Kerry and Monaghan, records show that the amount of money spent on emigration in Geashill was minimal. In his report to Lord Digby he listed those who left the estate between 1866 and 1870. He classed them as tenants, cottiers and those whose farms were re-let, noting that the total who left the estate in 1866 was 47, which included 10 members of the Dunne family from Killeenmore and nine members of the Warren family from Gorteen. Eight houses were levelled in the same year. The total who left in 1867 was 22. A further 23 left in 1868, while the totals for 1869 and 1870 were 12 and 24 respectively. He listed their destinations as Australia, New York, England and Scotland. However, these totals fall short of the drop in numbers recorded in the census for the corresponding period. It is therefore reasonable to conclude that the majority who left, or who were forced to leave, received little or no money from Trench; in fact in the 1864 annual report to Lord Digby he

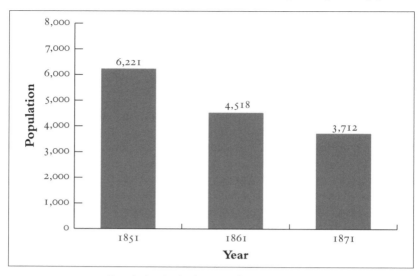

10 Population in the barony of Geashill, 1851–71.
Source: Census of Ireland, 1851, 1861, 1871

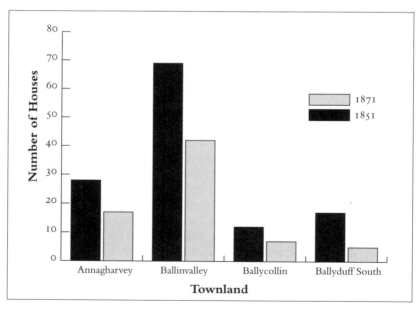

11 Bar chart showing the decrease in the number of houses in four selected townlands,
1851–71. *Source*: Census of Ireland, King's County, Barony of Geashill, 1851 and 1871

admitted that sons and daughters of small farmers and labourers had emigrated to America having had their passage paid by friends and relatives who had gone before them.[2]

Emigration to America, Australia and Britain increased during and in the aftermath of the Great Famine. In the mid-19th century Irish agriculture underwent a major transformation; farm size increased and both tillage and animal husbandry improved greatly. Such improvements benefitted a minority but for the lower class of farmers and labourers it meant leaving Ireland to escape the misery of poverty and the landlord oppression common on many Irish estates. For many it meant boarding a ship to America or Australia. Migration to Australia had been established since the beginning of the white settlement in New South Wales in 1788 and from 1830 the authorities there encouraged free or assisted immigration.[3] The northern area of New South Wales was declared a separate colony in December 1859 and the new authorities considered capital and labour a necessary requisite for economic development. They were therefore anxious to continue successful immigration schemes, especially from Britain where there was a search for small capitalists as well as agricultural and domestic workers. To entice immigrants the authorities agreed that all those who paid fares would be entitled to an £18 land order which could be redeemable for cash, which in turn could be used to purchase land. Initially these orders were transferable and so many shipping companies undertook the transfer of migrants. Others had family members pay their fares. However, for those who had no hope of raising the money, the Queensland Immigration Society was to provide assistance. The society was formed when Bishop Quinn, an Irish man and the then bishop of Queensland, was approached by a number of local Catholics to lead a support group for the suffering in Ireland.[4] They chartered ships to transfer the Irish destitute. Fr Paddy Dunne, an associate of Bishop Quinn and a native of Philipstown, now Daingean, played a leading role in the transfer of migrants from King's County especially from the barony of Geashill in the 1860s. Jennifer Harrison in her work titled *From King's County to Queensland* explains how Fr Dunne became aware that 'the able-bodied poor with their families were being evicted from the estate at Geashill and were crowding into the streets of Tullamore for shelter'.[5] They were homeless, penniless and near starvation. The parish and community were powerless to help them in their plight. Fr Dunne addressed meetings and ascended pulpits whenever he was allowed as sometimes there was strong opposition from the clergy. He arranged the funding and the safe passage of many tenants from the Geashill area by chartering ships such as *Erin go Breagh*, which brought many emigrants from Geashill and its surrounding hinterland to the new world.[6] According to local historian John Kearney, among those who left were families such as the Kellys from Ballina, Dempseys and Rafters from Ballycollin, Cruises from Killurin and Cuskellys from

Killerllery.[7] It seems that Geashill's geographical position was conducive to aiding emigration. Harrison attributes easy access to the Midland and Great Western Railways, part of which may be seen on the 1912 Ordnance Survey map of Geashill, as well as access to the Northern Railway as a major factor in facilitating movement to Queenstown (Cobh) from where many emigrant ships set sail.[8] The Midland and Great Western Railway passed through Geashill and a railway station was opened just outside the village in 1854 which operated for passenger travel until 1963.

Godkin in his chapter on lease-breaking in Geashill in his 1869 work on land in Ireland refers to many of the new school of land agents as political economists influenced by the demographer Thomas Malthus, who attributed most social problems to overpopulation and sought to rid the estates they managed of the 'Celtic race'.[9] Since Trench came from this new school of agents it seemed he too believed that many of the social problems at Geashill could be attributed to the peasants, whom he saw as 'lazy and thriftless' and who acted as a barrier to his plans for improvement. As a result, he adopted a hard-line authoritarian style of estate management. Some of the strategies employed by both William and Thomas Trench seem to back up this theory. Their first task was aimed at eliminating the numerous squatters who, under previous regimes had been allowed to establish themselves on the estate and who had not paid rent for more than 20 years. Their names in fact had never appeared on a rent book. These people had usually squatted along the side of the roads and lived in mud hovels with no windows and a hole in the roof, out of which stuck a piece of wickerwork, which made a chimney.[10] These vulnerable people put up little or no resistance and according to Trench were less difficult to remove than he had anticipated. He claimed he enticed them to leave by offering them between £5 and £20.[11] He suggested that they were quite happy with this arrangement. However, certain sources suggest that the Trenches adopted ruthless tactics to clear the estate of small tenants and beggars, in order to create larger holdings with better drainage and more advanced farming methods. Thomas Weldon Trench's treatment of a woman in Geashill village on Christmas eve 1861 illustrates this fact. While he was working on his estate in the village and acting in his capacity as local magistrate, he had an elderly woman, Jane Egan, aged 72, arrested for begging for a halfpenny.[12] It seemed that Trench constantly kept watch for vagrants and even carried a bible in his pocket in order to put under oath anyone whom he might wish to interrogate on suspicion of begging.[13] The case of Alice Dillon (Delin) illustrates just how ruthless Trench was. On the same day as Jane Egan was arrested, he noticed another elderly woman entering a local premises. On questioning the householder, he learned that the woman had asked for a cup of sugar. He immediately had the woman, Alice Dillon, who was 79 years old, arrested and incarcerated in Tullamore gaol, where she died, a few days later, while serving her sentence. An inquest into her death followed in Tullamore gaol on 3 January 1862.[14] Among those who gave evidence was Revd John Nolan, PP of Killeigh and Geashill. He told the court how he had called to the gaol to visit her on the 29 December and had found her dying. She told him she was dying and when he asked her what she believed was causing her death, she said, the journey to Tullamore gaol and the treatment she received there.[15] Another person who testified at the inquest was Patrick Payne, a sub-constable in the district of Geashill who said that on the 24 December Mr Trench called him and told him to take a woman into custody. Trench took a sworn statement from the owner of the premises at which Alice was arrested. He then instructed Mr Payne to take the accused to Tullamore gaol. Patrick Payne described the accused as being 'very feeble' and explained how she complained along the way of being very cold. When she was accused at the gaol, by Trench, she was 'near falling down'.[16] In his statement Mr Payne said he believed Alice Dillon to be 'a decent woman, this I heard from the people in my neighbourhood'.[17]

Local doctor, John S. Glover, from Phillipstown also gave evidence. He carried out an external examination on the deceased on 1 January and swore there was a mark over her right eye, a slight scar on the elbow of her right arm and an ulcer on her back. However, he suggested that these injuries were not sufficient to cause death and concluded that her death was caused by congestion of the lungs, common in people her age.[18] In the final results of the inquest an open verdict was returned. Fifteen out of 23 members of the jury agreed with the verdict that her death was caused by congestion of the lungs. The other eight were for finding her arrest and the journey to Tullamore gaol as factors in hastening her death. It is worth noting that all members of the jury were tenants at will (yearly tenants) on the Digby estate and perhaps a more objective jury would have found Trench guilty of a misdemeanour in this matter. The *Dublin Morning News* called on parliament to intervene in order to secure Trench's dismissal from the magistracy and one recent study suggests that only his strong links with Dublin Castle ensured that he remained a justice of the peace.[19]

Thomas Weldon Trench was, however, requested by the office of the lord chancellor to submit his version of events. In a letter to the lord chancellor, dated 11 February 1862,[20] he explained how between the hours of 11a.m.– 1p.m. on the day in question he observed a lady entering an open door of the local dispensary from the public street and that he had no doubt that she did so for the purpose of 'soliciting alms'. He explained how he inquired from a Miss Frances Carter, who lived in the dispensary, as to what the woman wanted. She confirmed the woman was begging. Trench went on to say he subsequently learned she requested a cup of sugar and when that was refused, she asked Miss Carter for money. The request was made immediately on the old woman crossing the threshold of the door and as she was then standing in a public place, he convicted her and sentenced her to one week in prison.[21] In reply, Trench received a letter from the lord chancellor's secretary. In the letter dated 4 March 1862, Trench was reprimanded for his harshness in the treatment of Alice Dillon. The secretary wrote, 'His Lordship feels bound to observe that your conduct on the occasion alluded to appears to him to be open to grave animadversion'. While the lord chancellor acknowledged that Trench may not have been unreasonable in his intent to carry out his duties against vagrancy in the locality, he did however accuse him of acting as 'a magistrate, prosecutor and judge'.[22] He went on to say that in the case of Alice Dillon,

> the conviction is plainly defective in not showing that she had committed such an act of vagrancy in a public place as would sustain it and the evidence against her did not establish the fact. The Lord Chancellor cannot adopt the view which you appear to entertain, that the passage of the dispensary house was a public passage with the meaning of the Act, which evidently refers to public streets or passages in the ordinary sense.[23]

The lord's chancellor's secretary noted that it was the opinion of the lord chancellor that the conviction of Alice Dillon was illegal both in form and substance and that the whole procedure was hasty and irregular: 'it had the appearance of great and unnecessary harshness and the conviction and the committal were both ill and irregular'.[24] He concluded the letter by informing Trench that the lord chancellor on that occasion would refrain from taking the extreme step of removing him as a commissioner of the peace. However, he cautioned him about his future as a magistrate and warned that the lord chancellor may not be as considerate 'if such misdemeanours re-occur'.[25]

The case of Alice Dillon illustrates the ruthlessness employed by the Trenches, especially Thomas Trench, towards the poorer people on the estate at Geashill. Had no public inquest been held, perhaps the Dillon case would have gone unrecorded. However, correspondence from the people of Geashill to Lord Digby also shows local discontent with Thomas Trench's behaviour in the barony. A letter written by a Flourida Hurst complained how Thomas Trench had her son arrested and imprisoned for shooting a wild bird on the estate. She claimed that her son was 'not the first or second victim of that man's ill will and imprisonment'.[26] By 1871 Thomas Weldon Trench resigned his post as resident agent in Geashill and was replaced by Lord Digby's nephew, Reginald Digby. One wonders if his position there had become so uncomfortable that he was forced to resign, as William Trench expressed great regret at his son leaving and implies that he may well have had no option but to do so. He explained to Lord Digby how he had looked forward with feelings of great satisfaction to having his son permanently located near his own home: 'it was mainly with a view to this and knowing his high qualities that I undertook the difficult, dangerous and responsible task of your lordship's agency when first you were good enough to offer it to me'.[27] In the annual report to Lord Digby he praised his son by referring to him as 'beloved and respected by the tenantry and looked up to and appreciated by all creeds, political or religious as a man of integrity, honour and intelligence',[28] a picture that greatly contradicts both the Dillon and Hurst stories.

Conclusion

The golden age of prosperity experienced in mid-Victorian Ireland was very much reflected on the Digby estate between 1857 and 1871 under the management of William Steuart Trench and his son Thomas. The fact that the Digbys were mainly absentee landlords may account for why the village of Geashill never actually developed into a town like neighbouring Birr/Parsonstown. It didn't acquire Georgian squares, courthouses or denominational churches, typical of other landlord estates in Ireland. However, there were vast improvements in both the architecture of Geashill village and the topography of the landscape in the barony during the Trench years. Such a metamorphosis earned Trench the legacy of an improver who was well ahead of his time. Yet, he is also remembered as a tyrant who broke leases, levelled huts, thinned the estate of much of its tenantry and in so doing was often ruthless in his style of management. This book sets out to establish what the true 'realities' were at Geashill under his management. There is no doubt that the work of William Steuart Trench and his son Thomas did result in great improvements to both the village of Geashill and to the Digby estate. So successful were these improvements that they gained both national and international recognition; Lord Digby was awarded the Hall Challenge Cup by the Royal Agricultural Society of Ireland for three successive years and in Paris in 1867 he won a bronze medal for the model of cottages built on his estate.[1]

The condition of any Irish estate depended on the amount of interest the landlord had in his property. As an absentee landlord, Lord Digby most likely invested the bulk of his money in his English properties where he resided, accounting for the fact that Geashill was never raised to 'town' status. However, he certainly displayed an ongoing interest in his Geashill estate and he was anxious to encourage advancements on other estates throughout the country. His willingness to donate the Digby Challenge Cup for land improvements to be presented by the Royal Agricultural Society of Ireland is evidence of this. His desire for improvement was perhaps no surprise given the fact that he was the grandson of Thomas Coke, who played an instrumental role in the Agricultural revolution in Britain almost a century earlier. Records of regular visits by Lord Digby to the estate during the 1860s suggest that he was certainly interested in the improvements that were implemented. Letters of thanks from local people to Lord and Lady Digby would also suggest that the local community appreciated his interest and contribution, for example a David Gorry wrote to him thanking him for the improvements to his home. In the correspondence he acknowledged the receipt of money received from Lord Digby to carry out such improvements and expressed a desire for the landlord to visit and see the improvements for himself.[2]

While Edward St Vincent Digby may have planted the seed for improvements carried out on his Irish property and displayed a keen interest in their progress, one cannot underestimate the contribution of William Steuart Trench to the transformation of Lord Digby's estate. It was he who was responsible for the planning and implementation of such improvements. Trench was a professional agent who brought much expertise to his post at Geashill; expertise which he had gained in previous employment on the Bath, Shirley and Lansdowne estates. In transforming the estate from one of the most wretched he had seen, where the attitude of the tenants was indifferent, summed up by the phrase 'let us alone', Trench and his son had to tackle first the problems of subdivision, arrears and lease-breaking. In dealing with such issues he embarked upon a clearing process which involved the removal of the 'worse characters' or 'weeding them out' to add their land to the farms of what he called the 'most improving tenants', namely Marcus Goodbody, a local businessman and Frederick Denning, a local bank manager.

In dealing with the problem of arrears Trench displayed some formidable characteristics by attempting to recognize the tenants who were reliable, offering to have 50 per cent of their arrears struck off immediately and offering yearly tenants a 75 per cent reduction. In an effort to solve the problem of lease-breaking on the estate, tenants were given compensation. These actions, although controversial, did help to ensure his control over the estate. In his dealing with these problems he eradicated small holdings and had small tenant farmers and paupers removed from the estate. Some he claimed were assisted by Lord Digby to emigrate to America and Australia. However, he admitted that sons and daughters of small farmers and labourers had emigrated to America having had their passage paid by friends and relatives who had gone before them.[3] Other emigrants were aided by a scheme introduced by a Fr Paddy Dunne, a native of Daingean parish. Overall, the population of Geashill declined by 40.3 per cent during the Trench years, suggesting that the age of improvement at Geashill came at a cost to the lower classes. These people he considered a barrier to improvement. The case of Alice Dillon illustrates how the actions of Thomas Weldon Trench were ruthless and hasty in dealing with the removal of a beggar woman. His actions were questioned by the Lord Chancellor, from whom he received a strong reprimand and warning,[4] an episode he omitted in the annual reports to Lord Digby and in his *Realities of Irish life*. The physical legacy of the Trench years was a positive one which resulted in a much improved estate with bigger and better quality farms, improved cottages, a new school and estate office. Such improvements however, did not bring contentment to the tenantry. In fact, they contributed to a flame of agitation and the rise of Ribbonism. So strong was this discontent that Trench was made aware of a plot to kill himself and his son.[5] Some of the incidents reported to Lord Digby appeared under the label of Ribbonism but were more likely to be the response of aggrieved tenants towards Trench's management. Other cases were somewhat convenient to his plans for clearance on the estate. This may well have been the case when the fire at the stables was attributed to Healion, a leading Ribbonman, whom Trench wished to remove. Other sources suggest that the fire was in fact caused by some of Trench's own staff at the castle.

In a gradual process between December 1871 and January 1872 Reginald Digby, Lord Digby's nephew, replaced the Trenches as land agent in Geashill.[6] Both Trench and his son Thomas Weldon died within a few days of each other in 1872 and were buried in Co. Monaghan. The decades which followed were to see Ireland plunged into a land war. Geashill, like elsewhere, would witness land agitation. The Land Commission was set up in 1881 and by 1903 the lands of Lord Digby were sold among the tenants. Geashill Manor which was home to successive agents was gutted by irregular forces during the civil war in August 1922.[7] The legacy of the Trenches lives on, and William Steuart Trench's legacy is that of an agent who created a golden age of prosperity in the barony. However, not all members of the community shared in this prosperity. The restructuring of this landed estate through the years has been greatly overshadowed by the realities of an agent who broke leases, levelled people's homes and banished the poor and in so doing was ruthless in his management of Lord Digby's estate. Trench's 'realities' were therefore not the only realities experienced at Geashill.

Notes

ABBREVIATIONS

HC   House of Commons
OAHS   Offaly Archaeological and Historical Society, Tullamore
PRONI   Public Records Office of Northern Ireland

INTRODUCTION

1 R.V. Comerford, 'Ireland 1850–70: post-Famine and mid-Victorian' in W.E. Vaughan (ed.), *A new history of Ireland*, vol. v (Oxford, 1989), p. 372.

2 Ibid. L.M. Cullen, *An economic history of Ireland since 1660* (London, 1971). James S. Donnelly, *The land and people of nineteenth-century Cork* (London, 1975). Terence Dooley, *The decline of the big house in Ireland* (Dublin, 2001). W.E. Vaughan, *Landlords and tenants in mid-Victorian Ireland* (Oxford, 1994).

3 Vaughan, *Landlords and tenants*, p. 5.

4 Dooley, *The decline of the big house in Ireland*, p. 11.

5 Vaughan, *Landlords and tenants*, p. 5.

6 *Returns for the year 1870 of the number of landed proprietors in each county classed according to residence*, HC 1872 (167), xvii, 775.

7 Gerard Lyne, *The Lansdowne estate in Kerry, under the agency of William Steuart Trench, 1842–72* (Dublin, 2001), p. lii.

8 Lyne, *The Lansdowne estate in Kerry*, p. lii.

9 Lyne, *The Lansdowne estate in Kerry*.

10 Patrick Duffy, 'Emigrants and the estate office in the mid-nineteenth century: a compassionate relationship?' in Margaret Crawford (ed.), *The hungry stream: essays on emigration and famine: proceedings of the conference held at the Ulster-American Folk Park*. (Belfast, 1997), pp 71–86.

11 Digby private collection, box on Geashill (Minterne, Dorset).

12 William Steuart Trench to Lord Digby, Annual Reports, 1857–71 (Minterne, Dorset).

13 William Steuart Trench, *Realities of Irish life* (London, 1869), p. 330.

1. THE DIGBYS AND THE APPOINTMENT OF WILLIAM STEUART TRENCH

1 Gerard Lyne, *The Lansdowne estate in Kerry, under the agency of William Steuart Trench, 1842–72* (Dublin, 2001), p. xlv.

2 Lyne, *The Lansdowne estate in Kerry*, p. xlvii.

3 William Steuart Trench, *Realities of Irish life* (London, 1869), p. 38.

4 Donnelly, *The land and people of nineteenth-century Cork*, p. 181.

5 Lyne, Lecture on the Lansdowne estate in Co. Kerry, at the OHAS (Tullamore, 21 September, 2010).

6 Unspecified, Nassau William Senior, *An Oxford professor visits Birr, 1852, 1858 and 1862* (OHAS. Tullamore, 2007).

7 PRONI, Trench papers D4141, p. 2.

8 Lyne, *The Lansdowne estate in Kerry*, p. xlvi.

9 Patrick J. Duffy, 'Assisted emigration from the Shirley estate 1843–54', *Clogher Record*, 14 (2), (1992) 19.

10 Duffy, 'Emigrants and the estate office in the mid-nineteenth century', p. 73.

11 Lyne, *The Lansdowne estate in Kerry*, p. liv.

12 Lyne, *The Lansdowne estate in Kerry*, p. liii.

13 Interview with Tom Davis at Portarlington, Co. Laois (October 2009).

14 Duffy, 'Emigrants and the estate office',
    p. 76.
15 Ibid., p. 74.
16 *Genealogical and Heraldic Dictionary of the
    Peerage and Baronies of the British Empire*
    (London, 1851), p. 221.
17 Grainne Breen, 'Landlordism in King's
    County in the mid-nineteenth century'
    in William Nolan and T.P. O'Neill (eds),
    Offaly: history and society (Dublin, 1998),
    p. 632.
18 Samuel Lewis, *A topographical dictionary of
    Ireland* (London, 1837).
19 William Steuart Trench, *Realities of Irish
    life* (London, 1869), p. 311.
20 John Wright, *Offaly one hundred years ago*
    (Tullamore, 1989), p. 217.
21 *Genealogical and heraldic dictionary,* p. 340.
22 Wright, *Offaly one hundred years ago,* p. 219.
23 Trench, *Realities of Irish life,* p. 312.
24 Digby private collection, box on
    Geashill (Minterne, Dorset).
25 Trench, *Realities of Irish life,* p. 313.
26 *Burke's Peerage and baronetage* (105th ed.,
    London, 1969–70), p. 102.
27 Trench, *Realities of Irish life,* p. 313.
28 Lord Digby to W.S. Trench, *Deed of
    Contract, 5 September, 1857.* Number, 21A
    (Tullamore, OHAS).
29 Charles Coote, *Statistical survey of the
    King's county* (Dublin, 1801), p. 135.
30 Arnold Horner, *Mapping Offaly in the early
    19th century with an atlas of William Larkin's
    map of King's county, 1890* (Bray, 2006), p. 41.
31 Samuel Lewis, *A topographical dictionary of
    Ireland* (London, 1837, reprinted,
    Tullamore in *An A–Z of Co. Offaly,*
    1999), p. 58
32 Trench to Digby, Annual Report, 1857,
    p. 5.
33 Ibid., p. 1.
34 Ibid., p. 4.
35 Ibid., p. 4.
36 Ibid., p. 32.
37 Ibid., p. 42.
38 Ibid., p. 5.
39 Ibid., p. 5.
40 Ibid., p. 6.
41 George Taylor and Andrew Skinner, *Road
    maps of Ireland* (London, 1778), number 85.
42 Trench to Digby, Annual Report, 1857,
    p. 31.
43 Ibid., p. 31.
44 Lyne, *The Lansdowne estate in Kerry,* p. 654.

45 Trench to Digby, Annual Report, 1857,
    p. 49.
46 Ibid., p. 49.
47 Ibid., p. 38.
48 Ibid., p. 11.
49 Ibid., p. 11.
50 John Kearney, *The long ridge* (Tullamore,
    1992), p. 94
51 James Godkin, *The land war in Ireland*
    (London, 1869), p. 354
52 Trench, *Realities of Irish life,* p. 316.
53 *Leinster Journal,* 23 Jan. 1858.
54 *The Nation,* 26 Jan. 1858.

2. CHALLENGES OF MANAGEMENT AT GEASHILL

1   Trench to Digby, Annual Report, 1857, p. 41.
2   Ibid., p. 39.
3   Ibid., p. 40.
4   Ibid., p. 40.
5   Ibid., p. 41.
6   Ibid., p. 42.
7   Ibid., p. 42.
8   Ibid., p. 42.
9   Ibid., p. 56.
10 Ibid., p. 56.
11 Ibid., p. 56.
12 Ibid., p. 56.
13 Ibid., p. 56.
14 Trench, *Realities of Irish life,* p. 323.
15 Trench to Digby, Annual Report, 1857, p. 45.
16 Trench to Digby, Annual Report, 1858, p. 2.
17 James Godkin, *The land war in Ireland*
    (London, 1869), p. 354.
18 Godkin, *The land war in Ireland,* p. 354.
19 Trench, *Realities of Irish life,* p. 316.
20 Ibid.
21 Trench to Digby, Annual Report, 1859.
22 Trench to Digby, Annual Report, 1858, p. 2.
23 Richard Griffith, *Primary valuation for the
    barony of Geashill, King's County* (Dublin,
    1854).
24 Trench to Digby, Annual Report, 1858,
    p. 2.
25 Trench, *Realities of Irish life,* p. 318.
26 Ibid.
27 Trench to Digby, Annual Report 1857, p. 2.
28 John Kearney, *The long ridge* (Tullamore,
    1992), p. 31.
29 Trench Digby, Annual Report, 1858
    (Minterne, Dorset).

30 Trench to Lord Digby, Annual Report, 1858, p. 146.
31 Ibid., p. 145.
32 Ibid., p. 145.
33 Trench, *Realities of Irish life*, p. 320.
34 *Leinster Journal*, 28 Jan. 1858.
35 Godkin, *The land war in Ireland,* p. 49.
36 Jennifer Kelly, '*The downfall of Hagan': Sligo Ribbonism in 1842* (Dublin, 2008), p. 11.
37 Trench, *Realities of Irish life*, p. 49.
38 Ibid., p. 324.
39 Godkin, *The land war in Ireland,* p. 349.
40 Ibid.
41 Trench, *Realities of Irish life.* p. 324.
42 Trench to Digby, Annual Report, 1860, p. 2.
43 Ibid., p. 25.
44 Ibid., p. 25.
45 Ibid., p. 25.
46 Ibid., p. 25.
47 Ibid., p. 27.
48 Nassau William Senior, *An Oxford professor visits Birr, 1858* (OHAS) 9 Jan. 2007.
49 Nesbitt to Trench, 21 Feb. 1860 (Minterne, Dorset).
50 Ibid.
51 Ibid.
52 Townsend Trench to his father, 10 Feb. 1860 (Minterne Dorset).
53 Ibid.
54 Ibid.
55 Trench to Lord Digby, Annual Report, 1860, p. 28.
56 Jennifer Harrison, 'From King's county to Queensland' in William Nolan (ed.), *Offaly: history and society* (Dublin, 2008), p. 735.
57 Thomas W. Trench to Lord Digby, 26 March 1860 (Minterne, Dorset).
58 F. Denning to Trench, 28 May 1862 (Minterne, Dorset).
59 Ibid.
60 Trench to Digby, Annual Report, 1862, p. 14.
61 Trench to Digby, Annual Report, 1860.
62 Trench to Digby, Annual Report, 1864.
63 Trench to Digby, Annual Report, 1868, p. 10.

3. IMPROVEMENTS ON THE ESTATE

1 Charles Coote, *Statitical survey of the King's County* (Dublin, 1801), p. 132.
2 Coote, *Statitical survey of the King's County*, p. 135.
3 Samuel Lewis, *A topographical dictionary of Ireland* (London, 1837, reprinted, Tullamore in *An A–Z of Co. Offaly,* 1999), p. 58.
4 Richard Griffith, *Primary valuation for the barony of Geashill, King's county* (Dublin, 1854), pp 158–9.
5 Patrick Duffy, *Exploring the history and heritage of Irish landscapes* (Dublin, 2007), p. 229.
6 Trench to Digby, Annual Report, p. 5.
7 Trench to Digby, Annual Report, 1861 (Minterne, Dorset).
8 Trench to Digby, Annual Report, 1869 (Minterne, Dorset), p. 55.
9 Trench to Digby, Annual Report, 1862 (Minterne, Dorset), p. 55.
10 Trench to Digby, Annual Report, 1871, p. 3.
11 *Genealogical and heraldic dictionary of the peerage and baronies of the British empire* (London, 1851), p. 213.
12 Report from the Royal agricultural society of Ireland, 25 May 1865 (Minterne, Dorset).
13 *Genealogical and heraldic dictionary of the peerage and baronies of the British Empire,* p. 213.
14 Trench, *Realities of Irish life,* p. 330.
15 *Census of Ireland 1871, pt I: Population–Leinster (C873–I to XIII),* HC1872 lxvii, p. 453.
16 Trench to Digby, Annual Report, 1861, p. 12.
17 Trench to Digby, Annual Report, 1861, p. 16.
18 Ibid.
19 *Census of Ireland 1871, pt I: Population–Leinster (C873-I to XIII),* HC1872 lxvii, p. 453.
20 Trench to Digby, Annual Report, 1863, p. 10.
21 Digby private collection, box on Geashill (Minterne, Dorset)
22 Trench to Digby, Annual Report, 1870, p. 9.
23 Ibid.
24 Trench to Digby, Annual Report, 1863.
25 Trench to Digby, Annual Report, 1858.
26 Trench to Digby, Annual Report, 1861, p. 15.
27 Trench to Digby, Annual Report, 1862, p. 5.
28 Ibid., p. 6.
29 Ibid., p. 6

30 Trench, *Realities of Irish life*, p. 328.
31 Ibid.
32 Ibid.
33 Trench to Digby, Annual Report, 1862, p. 6.
34 Ibid., p. 7.
35 Trench to Digby, Annual Report, 1861, p. 12.
36 Ibid., p. 12.
37 Ibid., p. 12.
38 Trench to Digby, Annual Report, 1862, p. 104.
39 Trench to Digby, Annual Report, 1861, p. 12.
40 Draining Geashill estate, report maps and costs, 1868 (OAHS).
41 Mary Pilkington, 'The campaign for rent reductions on the Digby estate, 1879–1882' in Rory Masterson (ed.), *Offaly heritage, vol. v* (Tullamore, 2008), p. 189.
42 Draining Geashill estate, report maps and costs, 1868.
43 Ibid.
44 Trench to Digby, Annual Report, 1869, p. 4.
45 Ibid., p. 54.
46 Ibid., p. 54.
47 Ibid., p. 4.
48 Trench to Digby, Annual Report, 1870, p. 4.
49 Ibid., p. 5.
50 Trench to Digby, Annual Report, 1871, p. 4.

7 John Kearney, *The long ridge* (Tullamore, 1992), p. 94.
8 Harrison, 'From King's county to Queensland', p. 737.
9 Godkin, *The land war in Ireland*.
10 Trench, *Realities of Irish life*, p. 327.
11 Ibid.
12 *Depositions at coroner's inquest at Tullamore, in King's county, Jan. 1862, on the body of Alice Delin, imprisoned in county gaol*, HC 1862 (377), xliv, 2.
13 *Inquest on Alice Delin*, xliv.
14 Ibid.
15 Ibid.
16 Ibid.
17 Ibid.
18 Ibid.
19 Pilkington, 'The campaign for rent reductions on the Digby estate, 1879–1882', p. 19.
20 *Inquest on Alice Delin*, xliv.
21 Ibid.
22 Ibid.
23 Ibid.
24 Ibid.
25 Ibid.
26 Letter from F. Hurst to Lord Digby, undated (Minterne, Dorset).
27 Trench to Digby, Annual Report, 1871, p. 5.
28 Ibid.

4. REALITIES FOR THE TENANTRY

1 *Census of Ireland 1871, pt I: Population–Leinster (C873–I to XIII)*, HC 1872, lxvii, p. 453.
2 Trench to Digby, Annual Report, 1864.
3 Jennifer Harrison, 'From King's county to Queensland' in William Nolan and T.P. O'Neill (eds), *Offaly: history and society* (Dublin, 1998), p. 739.
4 Harrison, 'From King's county to Queensland', p. 740.
5 Ibid., p. 745.
6 Ibid., p. 740.

CONCLUSION

1 *Genealogical and heraldic dictionary*, p. 213.
2 Letter from David Gorry to Lord Digby, Apr. 1869 (Minterne, Dorset).
3 Trench to Digby Annual report, 1864.
4 *Inquest on Alice Delin*, xliv.
5 Trench, *Realities of Irish life*, p. 324.
6 The Digby estate ledger, 1871–85, OAHS.
7 Dooley, *The decline of the big house in Ireland*, p. 191.